COMMUNICATION

FROM HIEROGLYPHS TO HYPERLINKS

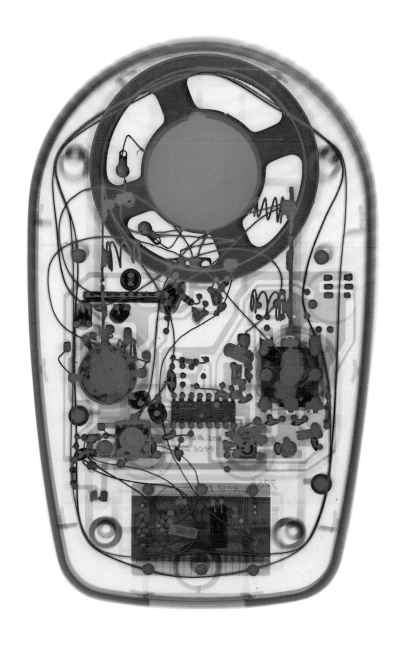

...ta. forte domini electionis numero
compleretur : sicutque paulus retumas
bone apostolicis actibus daret. qui sua
...creto strmulu recalcitrante. qui sua
sec. Quod et legentibus ac requirentibz
deu. et si per singula expediri a nobis
utile fuerat : sciens tamen op operario
agricolā oporteat de suis fructibus
dere. vitauim⁹ publicā curiositatē et
ne nō tā volentibz deū demōstrare uite
retur. quā fastidientibus prodidisse.
Explicat prefacio. Incipit euangeliū.
secundum lucā. Prohemium ipi̅ "
beati luce in euangelium suum

Q̇oniā quidē multi cō
nati sūt ordinare nar:
ratōnes q̄ in nobis com:
plete sūt rex. sicut tradi
derūt nobis q̄ ab inicio
ipi̅ viderūt. et ministri
fuerūt srmonis: visū ē et michi assecuto
ōnīa a pricipio dili gēter ex ordie tibi
scribere optie theophile : ut cognoscas
eor̄ verbor̄ de q̄bz erudit⁹ es veritatē.

Uit in diebus herodis re
gis iude sacerdos quidam
nomine zacharias de...

KINGFISHER KNOWLEDGE

COMMUNICATION
FROM HIEROGLYPHS TO HYPERLINKS

Richard Platt

Foreword by
The Honorable
Jonathan S. Adelstein

KINGFISHER
BOSTON

NOTE TO READERS

The web site addresses listed in this book are correct at the time of going to print. However, due to the ever-changing nature of the Internet, web site addresses and content can change. Web sites can contain links that are unsuitable for children. The publisher cannot be held responsible for changes in web site addresses or content or for information obtained through third-party web sites. We strongly advise that Internet searches are supervised by an adult.

Editor: Jennifer Schofield
Coordinating editor: Caitlin Doyle
Art director: Mike Davis
Cover designer: Mike Buckley
Picture manager: Cee Weston-Baker
Production controllers: Deborah Otter, Lindsey Scott
DTP manager: Nicky Studdart
DTP operator: Primrose Burton
Proofreader and Indexer: Jenny Siklos, Sheila Clewley

KINGFISHER
a Houghton Mifflin Company imprint
222 Berkeley Street
Boston, Massachusetts 02116
www.houghtonmifflinbooks.com

First published in 2004
10 9 8 7 6 5 4 3 2 1
1TR/0204/TWP/MA(MA)/130ENSOMA

ISBN 0-7534-5769-5
Copyright © Kingfisher Publications Plc 2004

LIBRARY OF CONGRESS CATALOGING-IN-PUBLICATION DATA
Platt, Richard.
   Communication / Richard Platt.
      p. cm.—(Kingfisher knowledge)
   Includes index.
   Summary: Explores the variety of ways in which humans communicate,
including flags and fires, speech and writing, and through use of electronic
media such as television and the Internet.
      1. Communication—Juvenile literature. [1. Communication.] I. Title. II. Series.

P91.2.P58 2004
302.2—dc22 2003061913

Printed in Singapore

GO FURTHER . . .
INFORMATION PANEL KEY:

 web sites and further reading

 career paths

 places to visit

◀ Thomas Edison (1847–1931) set up kinetoscope arcades where people could watch short movie clips at rows of coin-operated machines.

Contents

Foreword

Imagine a world without communication, a world where we have no means to express ourselves. Try to picture your life without telephones, cell phones, TV, radio, e-mail, or the Internet. For most of human history none of these were available. Every new development in technology dramatically improved our ability to interact. Each new phase created new connections between people and cultures.

Every person has a story to tell. Communication technologies bring us up-to-date with our friends and relatives and with the latest news from around the world. They enable each one of us to experience stories and images presented by others, as well as to share our creativity with a wider audience.

Yet, we often use communication tools routinely without thinking about how they work. Consider how early humans began with face-to-face gesturing and evolved to drawings and spoken words. They then interacted outside of their villages by transmitting stories and messages through smoke signals, mirrors, jungle drums, and carrier pigeons. This evolved to person-to-person telephone conversations, broadcast television, and Internet distribution. Today's exchanges are accomplished by digital packets of information transmitted over wires, radio waves, and even satellites. As technologies develop, each new step is marked by better quality signals, by faster and more efficient delivery, and by more portable and more innovative features.

Every communication device we use today has its own history. This book explores how far we have come. How would Alexander Graham Bell react to the phones of today? Did wireless architect Guglielmo Marconi realize that wireless technologies would become so widespread that most people would use them every day of their lives? Would early inventors of television technologies recognize the high-definition, plasma color televisions of today, given the enormous size and tiny screens of early televisions? While the rapid progress of their creations would astound each one of these pioneers, the Internet would amaze them even more. The Internet revolutionized communication like nothing ever has before, bringing the world to our fingertips.

By bridging physical distance, communication technologies transform communities and bring us closer. Think of Paul Revere's famous ride on horseback to alert his countrymen, "The English are coming!" and the many different ways he could alert communities today. At times governments have tried to harness the immense power of communication technologies for propaganda or censorship. We are fortunate that our society values the right of people to speak freely and encourages widespread access to communication technologies.

With all of the amazing ways to communicate today, communication technologies are still about helping people connect with one another, share ideas, and learn about the world around them. As you read, think about new ways you might find to express yourself. And just imagine the communication frontiers to come.

Jonathan Adelstein

The Honorable Jonathan S. Adelstein

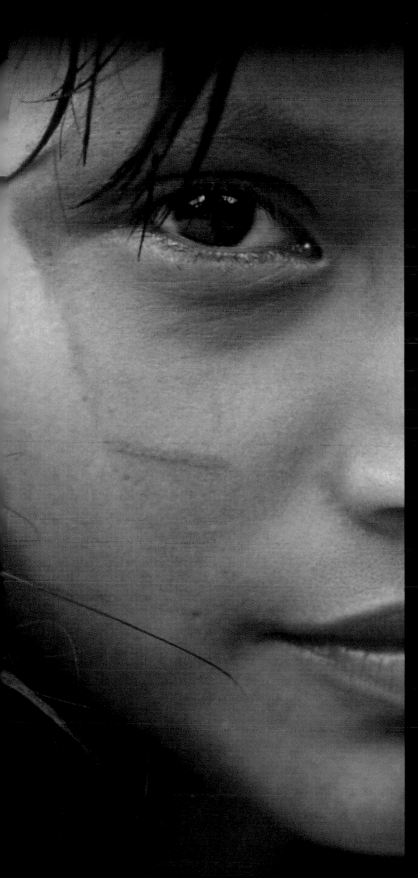

CHAPTER 1

Face-to-face

What is communication? It is a letter, a phone call, shouting, waving, and nodding. Do not forget television, radio, books, and newspapers. The list is long—much longer than you might think. People are not the only ones that communicate. Long before humans walked on Earth animals had solved the problem of communication. They used sound, color, taste, smell, and movement to send messages to each other.

We may think of speech as our simplest communication skill, but the first humans could not talk. Instead they grunted and used gestures. Even when people learned to speak, they never lost these basic, "no-words" communications skills. The next time you have a face-to-face conversation tune in to your animal side. You may express yourself better by punctuating your sentences with facial expressions and body language.

Just as speech began with grunts, pictures marked the dawn of written communication. Painted on cave walls or pressed in mud, they made a lasting record of messages. Picture writing is still used to break through language barriers— in a foreign city there is no mistaking the "paper doll" figure on a bathroom door.

Animal communication

Barking, buzzing, singing, and wagging, animals are far from silent. They may not be able to talk in words and sentences, but they never stop chattering. Instead they rely on scent, sound, light, color, and movement for signaling. They use messages to warn of danger, to lead their friends to food, for flirting with their mates, and for much, much more. In fact, communication in the animal world is so rich and varied that it makes humans look like the quiet ones. We mostly rely on our ears and eyes to communicate with each other, and although animals have powerful senses of hearing and sight, they also use smell and touch to send signals.

▲ By "dancing" in a figure eight pattern, a bee can tell other bees in the hive exactly where to find a rich source of food. The angle of the dance shows the direction of the food, and the quicker the dance, the closer the food.

Calling and crying

Animals use sound for signaling because sound travels long distances, and it can also work during the day or at night. However, sound fades very quickly, so it does not help hungry predators track and eat calling animals. It is also an adaptable way of signaling. By changing the volume, speed, and pitch, it is possible to make a huge variety of calls.

When a songbird spots a hungry cat, it sings a special "look out!" chirp that sends the other small birds zooming to safety. These warning songs are so specific that even humans can hear and recognize them. However, many other animal sound signals are in a form that we cannot understand—or even hear. For example, giant finback whales send messages with a sound that is too low in pitch for our ears to detect. And, at the other end of the musical scale, the squeaks made by bats are too high for us to hear.

▼ Humpback whales communicate with their mates using haunting "songs." The sequence of moans, chirps, cries, and snores is very loud and has been heard by sailors through the wooden hulls of ships. It sounded so strange that at least one crew abandoned their ship, convinced that it was haunted.

Apes use their expressive faces to communicate with each other. Some of their expressions look eerily like our own smiles and frowns, but their grimaces often have very different meanings from ours. For example a chimp's bare-teeth smile is a warning, not a greeting. Less advanced animals also use visual signals—think of a dog's wagging tail.

There are some animals that do not stop at just movement and actually change color to send messages. For instance the throat of the male stickleback—a spiny-finned fish—turns redder when he is angry or when he wants to attract a female. Tiny fireflies communicate in a similar way— they flash like lighthouses to signal that they are looking for mates.

▼ Chimpanzees are great communicators, using sounds, gestures, and expressions to chat in their African rain forest home. Captive chimps have learned to talk to people by signing us deaf people do or by pointing to pictures on a special keyboard.

Smelling and sniffing

Chemical communication— scents and tastes—does a very different task for animals. Unlike sounds, scents linger, so they are a useful way for mammals to leave marks that say "I live here—keep out." Insects that live in groups, such as ants, have a rich "language" of smells. They make scents to signal danger, to lay trails for other ants to follow, and to persuade other ants to groom them or carry them to safety when danger threatens.

Grinning and blushing

When they are close together, many animals use visual signals to send messages to each other.

Without words

Long before humans learned how to speak they were using their hands and faces to express themselves and pass on knowledge. Today we still rely on expressions and gestures to communicate our ideas to others. When we are talking, we grin and frown, raise our eyebrows, and stab at the air with fists and fingers to make a point. Even the way we sit can tell a different story from our words, revealing whether we are lying or telling the truth.

▶ We will never know how hominids used expressions and gestures to communicate before they learned how to speak. Studies of chimps—our closest nonhuman relatives—have not helped. Although many scientists have investigated chimp communication, no one understands more than a few words of "chimp speak."

Before speech

What makes us human? Most scientists agree that speech is one of the key abilities that separates us from our ape cousins. But the change from ape to human was slow, and the in-between beast probably used a language full of grunts, hand signals, and gestures. Like today's mimes, these early people found ways to get their meaning across without using speech.

Grimaces

Our facial expressions "speak" as clearly as our voices, and sometimes these expressions give away emotions we would rather hide. For example, when a person is standing calmly but they are tapping their foot, it is a sign that they are not calm at all.

Most of the time we use facial expressions to help a conversation along. We express disbelief by raising our eyebrows; surprise by opening up our eyes wide and mouth wide; delight by smiling—and all without interrupting the person who is talking.

Body language

Even when we are sitting still, we send off signals with our posture (the position of our body, arms, and legs). It is not too difficult to guess what others are thinking by studying their body language. For example, folding your arms during a discussion or an argument makes a barrier that means "I do not agree" or "I am not listening to you." If someone touches or hides their mouth while they are talking, it often means that they are not telling the truth. Leaning back, with your hands behind your head,

suggests "I am smarter than you," but leaning forward can mean "Should we get started?"

Experts in interviewing and questioning people, such as detectives, use body language to seek out the truth. We all use clues like these without actually realizing that we are doing it. For example, when we have a hunch that someone is not being completely honest, it is often because their words and their posture are saying different things.

Body language may be useful, but it is not foolproof. A man who keeps touching his mouth, for example, may not be lying—he may just have cut himself while shaving.

Hand signals

Next time you have an argument, try sitting on your hands. You will be surprised by how much you miss them. Although we use our hands all the time when we talk, not all of the gestures we use mean something. Some—like pounding the table— just make our words seem more important, but other gestures help us explain what we are saying. Pointing, for example, helps make it clear who or what we are talking about, and a clenched fist often shows anger more clearly than words ever could.

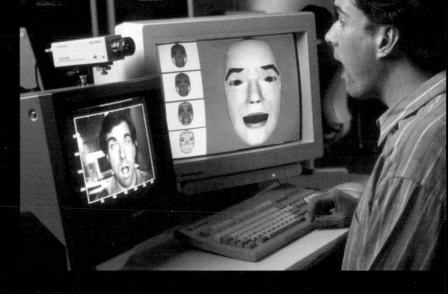

▲ Researchers seeking to understand human emotions have programmed computers to recognize them. Here a camera captures an open-mouthed "wow!" look; the computer recognizes it and makes a virtual copy of the face on screen.

▲ Some gestures, such as thumbs up for "okay," mean the same thing everywhere. Long ago a pointing finger to show travelers where to go was carved on road signs, but in an argument it accuses the person it is pointed at.

▼ Although shouting does not always win an argument, the loudness of our speech can help emphasize (stress) what we are saying. On the other hand, speaking quietly encourages the person listening to lean forward and pay closer attention to what we are saying.

▶ 800,000-year-old skulls dug up in Java, Indonesia, have bulges above the part of the brain that controls speech. This suggests that they are the remains of people who could talk. There is also evidence that these people made long sea journeys, which would have been difficult to organize if they could not talk.

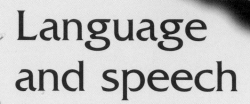

Language and speech

Speech is one of the most adaptable and powerful ways of communicating. We can shout a quick warning without a moment of hesitation. But with thought, preparation, and care, we can use speech to explain difficult and complex ideas. We can even "talk people around" to our point of view. However, learning to speak is not easy—our distant ancestors never managed to do it—and most of us celebrate our first birthday before we can speak our first word.

▼ Stephen Hawking (born 1942) is handicapped by motor neurone disease (MND)—an illness that affects muscles, including those in the throat. Although MND took away his ability to talk, Hawking has become one of the world's greatest physicists. He uses a computer with a special speech synthesizer in order to explain and dictate his clever ideas.

When humans began to speak

If fossils preserved words as well as they preserve the bones of our ancestors, we would know exactly when humans first learned how to speak. Unfortunately they do not, and the scientists who dig up ancient skeletons from the ground have found very few clues about how these early people communicated with each other.

It is not surprising that scientists disagree about when humans first learned how to speak. Although some think that the ability to talk is around 800,000 years old, there are other scientists who believe that we were all dumb (without speech) until around 300,000 years ago.

Skulls and ships

The scientists who believe in the more recent date of the two use the small skulls of ancient people as their evidence. They argue that the brains of our oldest ancestors were tiny and that they simply did not have the "brain power" to learn how to talk. Skull shapes also show the position of the larynx (the voice box in the throat that enables us to form words). If it is located too high up in the throat, the ability to speak is impossible. However, what these ancient people *did* tells a very different story. Around 800,000 years ago some of these people crossed wide oceans—how could they build and sail ships without talking to each other?

Learning to speak

We learn how to talk by listening to others and imitating them. Although most babies understand a few words by the time they are one year old, talking only comes a few months later. This is because they need to practice controlling the speaking equipment in their mouths (such as the tongue and lips) and the equipment in their throats (such as the larynx). Most babies say their first words between 12 and 18 months old and can form sentences of three or more words by the time they are two years old.

What is surprising about learning how to speak is that we only have one chance to do it. Scientists believe that if we have not mastered speech by the time we are teenagers, we will never really manage it. Raising a child in silence to prove this would be a cruel experiment. However, there are children who have been brought up by animals who did not hear speech when they were young. These children who first met other humans after the age of 12 rarely learned to speak more than a few words.

Speech therapy

Very few people have had to suffer in this way. However, there are as many as one in ten humans who have difficulty communicating through speech. Most of these people have lost the ability to speak through an accident or illness. Fortunately speech therapists can often help improve or sometimes even restore their speech. Where therapists fail to do this, patients are given speech synthesizers and other aids—giving them their lost voices back.

◀ "Wolf children" are children who cannot talk because they have never heard speech in order to be able to imitate it. Some wolf children have been raised by animals, although not always wolves, and others had parents who did not talk to them. Such handicaps are rare, and fewer than 50 wolf children have been found since 1900.

▲ Cave paintings, such as this example from the Cave of the Arrows in Mexico, often show the animals that the hunters of the time wanted to catch. Humans appear in this painting, but they are rare in the world's oldest cave paintings, which are found in southern Europe.

Writing it down

Talking is a quick way to tell someone what you are thinking, but the message is gone as soon as the echoes of your words fade away. In order to make your communications last, you need to record them—by carving, scratching, painting, pressing, or printing. Written messages began on cave walls with Stone Age pictures of prancing antelope and fearsome mammoths. In Asia, Africa, and the Americas scribes (writing experts) made these rough drawings into written languages. They used the new writing to record their stories, their history—and receipts for beer!

Painting cave walls

Prehistoric people started painting on the walls of caves 30,000 years ago. They used charcoal, mud, and sometimes even their own blood to create vivid scenes of animals and hunters. Often the painters climbed far below the ground to paint pictures in places that few people visited. It is difficult to tell why these pictures were made. Archaeologists cannot agree whether the paintings were just decorative or if they had a magic, lucky meaning. But whatever their use, these cave paintings mark the beginning of written communication.

Earliest known writing

The next big step forward was the invention of writing in Sumer (modern-day Iraq). In 3300 B.C. the Sumerians began scratching and pressing messages into flat lumps of soft clay. At first they used tiny pictures to represent different objects and ideas. But gradually these pictures looked less and less like the objects they represented. Eventually Sumerian scribes gave up drawing these intricate pictures and turned their marks into standard signs, with each sign standing for a whole word. The scribes used the wedge-shaped end of a cut reed as a stylus (writing tool) and created a type of writing known as cuneiform. The writing was so successful that the Sumerians' neighbors also began to use it.

▼ Scribes of Sumer pressed the world's oldest adventure story into soft clay around 4,000 years ago. In the story the hero Gilgamesh (below) attacks a fire-breathing monster whose gaze turns men into stone. The cuneiform writing that scribes used makes up the background of this page.

A few ancient Egyptian signs stood for sounds as well as objects. For example, the blue worm at the bottom of this message could mean both the letter "f" and a horned viper—a small, very poisonous desert snake.

Many of the clay tablets that the Sumerians created still exist. Although some are business records, such as beer receipts, the Sumerians also used cuneiform to create the world's first superhero story—the epic of Gilgamesh.

Picture writing improved

Outside of Sumer scribes found other ways to adapt and improve pictures so that they could record language. In Egypt the pictures were simpler. They also used a few of them to stand for some of the sounds of speech, just as we use letters today. The result was hieroglyphic writing, which the Egyptian scribes began to use 5,000 years ago. Within three centuries the Egyptians had devised quicker ways of writing, but they kept hieroglyphics for important and special messages until around A.D. 400.

Elsewhere in the world picture writing thrived. When Spanish adventurers traveled to Central America in the A.D. 1500s, they discovered that the Aztec people who ruled Mexico also used pictures for writing. Their written language looked a little like the Egyptians' hieroglyphics, although the two types of writing developed 3,500 years and 7,440 mi. (12,000km) apart.

Modern picture writing

In some Asian countries, such as Japan and China, people still write using small pictures. Many pictures stand for a whole word, and there have to be many signs to represent every object or idea. Writing in Chinese, for example, involves learning around 4,000 pictures. Most of the pictures have been simplified so that they are quicker to write, making their meaning hard to guess from the sign, but some are easy to recognize such as the Japanese sign that looks like an open umbrella—and means exactly that.

▶ Aztec priests used picture writing like this to record Mexico's history, details of temple ceremonies, and tax demands. Although the Aztecs' written language had few words, this did not matter—priests used the writing like notes, filling in the details from memory.

SUMMARY OF CHAPTER 1: FACE-TO-FACE

The dawn of communication

Communication began long before human beings walked on Earth. Animals used sound, movement, color change, scent, and taste to send messages to each other. Our ape ancestors became experts at communication, and when humans evolved from them, we developed their communication skills even further. At first humans could not speak but instead used the apes' sounds, expressions, and gestures to get the message across. We still use these grimaces to emphasize our words. We smile and frown or raise our eyebrows to express surprise, and we wave our hands around when we are excited. We also send subtle signals about our mood, using our arms, legs, and bodies.

People probably learned to talk more than 300,000 years ago. Experts cannot agree about the exact date, but judging by what people achieved in the distant past, they were communicating effectively much earlier than this. However, the evidence from fossilized skulls suggests that we learned to speak more recently than this.

Learning to talk

Children learn how to speak by listening to adults and imitating what they hear. Few babies can talk much before their first birthday. Even after their first words, learning to form complete sentences is a slow process. Children raised in silence rarely learn to speak fluently, and even if they hear speech later on in life, they often find it impossible to learn more than just a few words.

Although talking is a quick way to communicate, words do not last, and people began making permanent records around 30,000 years ago. They started by painting images on cave walls. These showed the animals that they hunted and occasionally human figures. The first writing used pictures, too, although they were smaller and simpler than cave paintings. Writing began around 5,000 years ago, when the Sumerians used cut reeds to scratch and press pictures into damp clay. The people of Egypt carved and painted a form of picture writing that we call hieroglyphics.

Other people around the world also developed their own picture writing systems, and today Chinese and Japanese characters are still based on pictures.

Go further . . .

Mix your own music using animal sounds:
www.nhm.ac.uk/interactive/sounds

Write your name in hieroglyphs:
www.upennmuseum.com/hieroglyphsreal.cgi

Learn how British charity ICAN is helping children communicate:
www.ican.org.uk

How Animals Communicate by Bobbie Kalman (Crabtree Publishing Co., 1996)

Decoding Egyptian Hieroglyphs: How to Read the Secret Language of the Pharaohs by Bridget McDermott (Chronicle, 2001)

Anthropologist
Although anthropologists study human origins and culture, some specialize in primate communication.

Archaeologist
Studies peoples and cultures from history using inscriptions and wall paintings.

Historical linguist
Investigates languages used in the past, including the understanding and translation of nonalphabetic writing systems.

Speech therapist
Helps people suffering from speech impediments, such as stammers, communicate more effectively.

See hieroglyphs and the Rosetta stone at:
The British Museum
London, England WC1B
Phone: 44 20 7323 8299
www.thebritishmuseum.ac.uk

Visit the Pony Express Museum at:
914 Penn Street
Saint Joseph, MO 64503
Phone: (816) 279-5059
www.ponyexpress.org

Visit a cave in France containing some of the world's most famous wall paintings:
Lascaux Cave, Montignac
Dordogne, France
Phone: 33 5 53 35 50 10
www.culture.gouv.fr:80/culture/arcnat/lascaux/en/index3.html

CHAPTER 2

From me to you

For a long time communication was only person to person. If you wanted to send a letter, a messenger had to carry it for you. Postal services made things simpler—but not much quicker—because the letter still had to travel by horse-drawn carriage to its final destination.

Flashing signals or flapping flags were faster than horses, but hilltop beacons cannot say much more than "yes" or "no," and even the best visual signal travels only as far as the eye can see.

The discovery of electricity changed this. Telegraph wires buzzed, not with speech but with pulses of power. Soon telephone calls replaced this code of "dots and dashes." In at least one way these calls are like the written messages of the past—they are still me-to-you signals. And nothing brings people closer than a one-on-one, personal message.

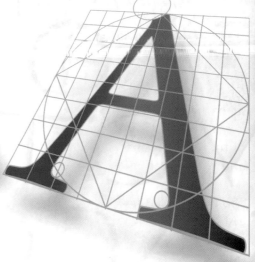

▶ As people adapted the alphabet to suit their own language, they changed the letters a little. Here is the letter "A" written in Semitic script, ancient Greek, and our own Roman alphabet. The green grid shows how circles and straight lines create the letter's shape.

Alphabets

Once we have the hang of reading and writing, nothing seems simpler. No wonder we say things are "as easy as A-B-C." However, inventing the alphabet was not easy at all. The change from picture writing systems to the letters that we use today began around 3,000 years ago. Our alphabet was not finished until the A.D. 1000s, when scribes added "W" to complete the Roman alphabet's 26 letters.

◀ Although the Arabic alphabet also developed from the Semitic—and like ours, has 26 letters—the shape of the letters changes according to whether they are at the beginning, the middle, or the end of the word.

Why not just use pictures?

The advantages of an alphabet over a picture writing system seem obvious to us now. Pictures stand for words or ideas, so writers need to learn hundreds of them before they can write. But in an alphabet each letter stands for a single sound. In English—with 26 letters—it is possible to write anything we can say out loud. However, when picture writing was the *only* way of writing, nobody noticed its drawbacks.

What, no vowels?

The first people to write using letters were probably the Phoenicians, who lived on the eastern coast of the Mediterranean Sea. In the 1000s B.C. they began to write what we now call Semitic script. Although their alphabet had 22 letters, it lacked the vowels "A," "E," "I," "O," and "U."

Borrowing the alphabet

The Phoenicians were a great seafaring nation, and it may have been their mariners who took the Semitic alphabet to Greece. The Greeks quickly understood its advantages and adapted it to suit their own language. The Semitic alphabet had more consonants than the Greek alphabet, so the Greeks had consonants to spare. They used these leftover consonants to stand for vowel sounds and created the first full alphabet between 1000 and 900 B.C. Greek letters also gave the alphabet its name—the word "alphabet" is made by linking the first letter of the Greek alphabet, "alpha," and the second letter, "beta."

The Roman alphabet

Just as the Greeks borrowed letters from the Phoenicians to write their own language, the Etruscan people of Italy borrowed from the Greeks. They began using an alphabet in the 700s B.C. The people of Rome used and improved the Etruscan alphabet. They used the letters "A," "B," "E," "H," "I," "K," "M," "N," "O," "T," "X," and "Z" exactly as the Greeks had. The Romans also adapted other Greek letters to add "C," "D," "G," "L," "P," "R," "S," and "Y." The letters "F," "V," and "Q" were no longer used in Greek, but the Romans thought that they were useful and put them back into use. This gave us most of the letters we use today to write in English.

Adding the finishing touches

The English alphabet has 26 letters, but the Roman alphabet only had 23. European scribes added "J," "U," and "W" between the A.D. 500s and 1000s. Even as recently as the 1800s some books still used "I" and "J" interchangeably. Although we can trace the roots of our alphabet back 3,000 years, it was perfected less than 200 years ago.

The way that the Roman alphabet is written has also changed. The Romans started with just capital letters. Writing developed slowly from these capitals. Roman writers adapted the capital letters a little to make them easier to read. However, by the A.D. 700s monks copying Bibles and other religious books had devised a completely new way of writing, called "minuscule." During the centuries that followed this flowing, curving handwriting style became the small letters we use today.

▲ We write in English from left to right, but Arabic writing goes from right to left. Some Asian languages go up and down the page, and this Greek writing from 450 B.C. even changes direction every other line!

▼ Romans often wrote on wooden boards coated in wax. Although the wax has disappeared from the boards that have survived, it is still possible to read some of the letters where a heavy hand pressed them through onto the wood.

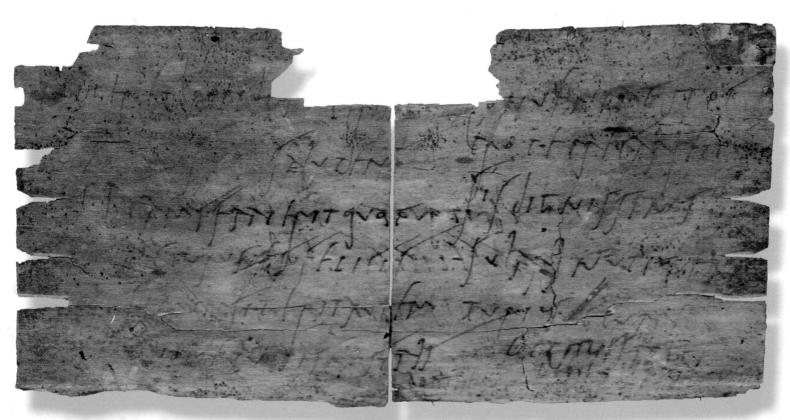

► Marco Polo (1254–1324) visited China when it was ruled by the Mongols. They were famous for their horseback riding ability, and today people from Mongolia keep the traditions alive of the mounted messengers that fascinated Marco Polo.

▼ Troops in World War II (1939–1945) used pigeons to send messages from areas of intense fighting to distant control centers. The birds flew through fog, smoke, bullets, and dust, delivering information when every other method failed.

Messengers

More than 2,500 years ago Pheidippides—history's most famous messenger—ran 25 mi. (40km) with the news of a Greek victory at the battle of Marathon. It is not surprising that after delivering the message he died from exhaustion! In the centuries that followed few messengers have been as dedicated—although the information they carried was just as urgent. Until postal services began servants carried important messages personally, traveling on foot or on horseback to deliver news.

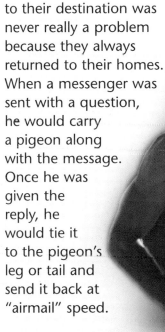

Riders and runners

Official messenger services began during the great empires of the past. Government messengers hurried to deliver urgent news in Egypt 4,000 years ago, as well as 1,000 years later in China. The Chinese messengers still ran an efficient service when a Venetian traveler, Marco Polo, visited the country in the 1200s. He reported that a relay of messengers on horseback carried urgent news up to 248 mi. (400km) in one day.

Chinese runners also carried messages, each one racing 3 mi. (5km) at a time. Bells attached to their belts signaled their arrival so that the next runner in the relay could be ready to take the letter and race onward. Aside from the letters, the runners also brought the emperor ripe fruits from the warmest parts of China.

Roman messengers

The rulers of ancient Rome also needed a messenger service in order to control their huge empire, which was spread out over most of Europe and beyond. Their *cursus publicus* (state runners service) used a series of rest houses spaced 7.5 mi. (12km) apart on main roads. During brief stops messengers would swap their exhausted horses for rested ones before galloping away with the mail.

In the A.D. 400s the Roman Empire collapsed. The well-made roads broke up into muddy trails, and many of Europe's small countries did not need the messenger service of a mighty empire. Eventually the *cursus publicus* ceased to run.

Guilds and merchants

With the rise of guilds (business companies) in the 1200s, messengers were once again in demand. They carried letters for wealthy merchants in Italy. Similar messenger services began in Great Britain, France, and other European countries. Not only did the messengers take information and news between the many great fairs where merchants gathered, but they also went farther afield to places such as Constantinople (modern-day Istanbul) and Persia (modern-day Iran).

Airmail with a beak

Messages were not always delivered by humans. Since the time of the Egyptian pharaoh Rameses III (1198–1167 B.C.) pigeons have carried messages much faster than the swiftest runners. Guiding the birds to their destination was never really a problem because they always returned to their homes. When a messenger was sent with a question, he would carry a pigeon along with the message. Once he was given the reply, he would tie it to the pigeon's leg or tail and send it back at "airmail" speed.

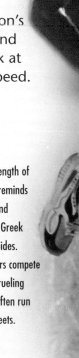

▶ The name and length of the marathon race reminds us of the sacrifice and achievement of the Greek messenger Pheidippides. Thousands of runners compete to finish first in a grueling contest, which is often run through city streets.

▲ Have you ever wondered what happens to your letter after you put it in a mailbox? From the mailbox your letter is picked up and transported by truck to a sorting office.

▼ Mail coaches traveled twice the speed of the mail boys they replaced, zooming along at an alarming 11 mph (17km/h). Their journeys were not always smooth— bad roads delayed them, and armed highwaymen stopped the coaches and stole the mail.

◀ At the regional center machines cancel the stamps and sort the mail by destination regions.

▲ Most domestic mail is taken to the regional sorting office by truck, but airmail is moved by aircraft to the destination country.

The postal service

Mailing a letter is so easy and familiar to us that we rarely think about what an amazing service we are using. When the post office delivers our mail to anywhere in the country—or in the world—it usually arrives within a few days, and the cost is relatively inexpensive—no matter how far the letter travels. However, it has not always been this easy or cheap. When postal services began in England and France, letters were a very expensive luxury that only the rich could afford to send.

▲ Famous riders of the Wild West worked for the Pony Express service. Calamity Jane (Martha Jane Cannary, 1852– 1903) rode for the company, and Buffalo Bill (William Cody, 1846–1914) was just 15 years old when he delivered mail.

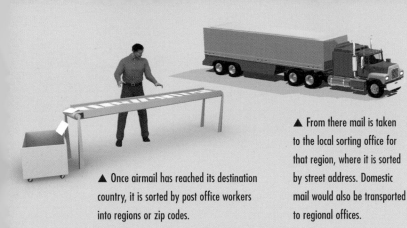

▲ Once airmail has reached its destination country, it is sorted by post office workers into regions or zip codes.

▲ From there mail is taken to the local sorting office for that region, where it is sorted by street address. Domestic mail would also be transported to regional offices.

▲ Mail carriers then pick up their mail from the sorting office.

▲ All mail is then hand delivered to mailboxes.

First post

The first postal service was started in 1464 by King Louis XI of France. In Great Britain, 50 years later, the king set up a service for royal letters. The horse-riding mail boys were not supposed to deliver letters for anyone else, but they did, and in 1581 an official public postal service began.

The mail boys were slow and often drank too much alcohol, and at the end of the 1700s fast mail coaches replaced them. The coaches sped along, stopping at rest houses to change horses. Mailing a letter was expensive. Delivery was charged by distance—sending a letter 8 mi. (13km) cost a manual laborer a whole day's pay.

American letters

Most of the American colonies (modern-day U.S.) had postal services by 1700, but as settlers spread out west across the continent, delivery times became longer and longer. Special high-speed services tried to change this. The best known was the Pony Express, which linked Missouri and California.

Despite its fame, the company never made money, and within 18 months the electric telegraph (see page 26) put the riders out of work.

Penny post

Modern "one-price" postal services began in England in 1837. Rowland Hill (1795–1879) showed that delivering a letter around the corner cost the post office almost as much as sending it the length of the country. He suggested a single price for letters of one penny to be paid by buying a stamp. At the time the average price was six times higher, and the person receiving the letter had to pay the mail carrier on delivery. Hill's "penny post" was a great success, and the number of letters mailed quickly paid for the cut-rate service. Many other countries copied it too, starting with Switzerland and Brazil.

Mailing letters overseas remained a problem until an international postal treaty in 1878. Since then sending a letter across the world only needed a single stamp, no matter how many countries it passed through.

▶ Street mailboxes were first found in Paris, France, in 1653, but they were not an immediate success. People put garbage through the slots, and mice crept inside and gnawed the mail.

Flags and fires

A blazing beacon or a smoky fire may not seem like the most obvious way to communicate, but when you just want to say "yes" or "no," these flaming signals are the quickest way to spread the news. They are also instantly visible from far away, so people have used them to send long-distance messages since ancient times. Fire carries only simple information, but there are other visual signals that are more versatile. Flags, for example, can spell out whole sentences to those who understand their colorful code, and the reflection of mirrors can be used to send sentences over great distances.

◄ Just one or two flags are enough to send signals—as long as the person who is receiving the message can clearly see the position of the flags. Wigwag signaling uses a single flag, and semaphore signaling uses two flags—one held in each hand. This sailor is signaling the letter "e" in semaphore.

► By holding a blanket over a smoking fire and then lifting it, Native Americans created signals from puffs of smoke. A single puff meant "attention!," while three puffs in a row was the signal for danger.

Speedy beacons

A signal can easily speed along a chain of beacons in the time it takes to light a fire, and the higher a beacon is, the farther away it can be seen. More than 3,200 years ago the Greeks built beacons to send signals from the city of Troy to their capital Mycenae, a huge distance away. The flame of one beacon at the top of a 6,560-ft. (2,000-m)-high mountain could be seen 112 mi. (180km) away.

Fire and smoke

Native Americans improved existing flame communications so that they could use smoky fires to send more than just simple "yes" and "no" signals. By changing the number of fires and the spacing between them, they signaled their safe arrival at the end of a journey, an emergency, or how many enemies a war party had killed.

Shining mirrors

In the 1800s there was conflict over land between Native Americans and white Americans. An American army

general, Nelson Miles (1835–1925), sent to Arizona to defeat the Native Americans quickly saw the value of visual signals in the clear desert air. Reflecting sunlight from mirrors, his men sent bright flashes to observers up to 30 mi. (50km) away. By using the dots and dashes of Morse code (see page 26), they could easily transmit a 16-word message in one minute.

▶ Today many naval ships keep signal flags for decoration. But in the days of sailing ships using different colored flags was the only way to send a message to a vessel that was too far away to shout to. In this example the red flag with the yellow cross stands for the letter "r."

Flapping a message

The Greeks were using flags to send messages 2,400 years ago. However, flags were not used for advanced signaling until the 1700s, when the French navy devised a cunning flag code. This assigned numbers to the 1,000 most common messages. Different flags represented the numbers 0 to 9, so hoisting three flags up to the masthead of a ship could quickly send a signal to the whole fleet. Other navies improved the idea with flags representing each letter. For example, the English flag code "AS" meant "My ship has struck the rocks and is breaking apart."

◀ Claude Chappe's telegraph network carried messages all over France. Towers were spaced approximately 6 mi. (10km) apart, and two signalers worked in each tower. One signaler watched the neighboring tower through a telescope and called out the signals to his partner. The partner would then move the signaling arms on the roof of the tower, sending the message to the next tower.

Claude's telegraph

One of the most clever methods of visual signaling was a French invention by Abbot Claude Chappe (1763–1805). He suggested building a network of towers, each one with a movable H-shaped signal on top. Controls inside the tower adjusted the angles of the "legs" and "crossbar" of the "H" in a code that stood for letters of the alphabet. Each tower was in sight of two others—signalers inside watched their neighbors and copied the messages. With this "pass-it-on" system, messages could travel 71 mi. (115km) in one minute.

Electric telegraph

In 1860 an urgent message took ten days to cross the United States in the saddlebags of a galloping pony. The following year the same message took just minutes to arrive. This is because in 1861 telegraph wires linked the east and west coasts of the United States for the first time. The wires crackled not with speech but with long and short pulses of electrical power. This code of dots and dashes was named after Samuel Morse, the American artist who had helped perfect the telegraph 25 years earlier.

▲ The tugboat *Goliath* laid the first underwater telegraph cable across the English Channel in 1850. Although it broke within a week, a thicker cable that was laid two years later was a success.

▼ Morse wanted the telegraph to transmit only numbers 0–9, but Alfred Vail persuaded him to use a code of short pulses (dots) and long ones (dashes) for the alphabet. For example, ··· ·· ·· ··· · ···· ·· ··· ··· ··· · spells out Samuel Morse.

The doorbell that talked

The telegraph worked like a doorbell—pressing a button closed a switch; the switch let power flow in an electric circuit; the power operated a buzzer. What made the telegraph different was that the button and buzzer were miles apart. And with Morse code, the button signaled more than "let me in." It sent 30 words per minute whizzing down the wires.

Samuel Morse (1791–1872) did not invent this clever system, nor did he invent the code named after him. But he made the telegraph a success. He was so sure that it was the best way to communicate that he worked hard to wire up the entire U.S.

Morse had help

Morse was not a scientist, and his first try at building a telegraph failed. It could not send signals across a room, let alone across the country. In order to get the system

◄ The telegraph gave American leaders instant news of victories and defeats during the Civil War (1861–1865). Mobile telegraph units, such as this one, laid enough cable to stretch halfway around the world.

▼ Telegraph operators tapped a key in order to send messages. At the receiving station a machine printed the message out, but operators soon learned to "read" the signal by listening to the clicks of the printer.

working, he called on chemistry professor Leonard Gail and student Alfred Vail. Together they tested it by winding 10 mi. (16km) of wires around a room.

Morse, Gail, and Vail showed their telegraph to officials in Washington, D.C. The officials were impressed, and the partners won a grant of $30,000 to build a telegraph line linking the city to Baltimore, Maryland, 40 mi. (65km) away. The next year saw lines link New York City to four other cities. A frenzy of telegraph-line building followed, and the network doubled in size every seven months.

Going global

This enthusiasm was found in other countries, too, as enterprising companies rushed to raise telegraph poles. Copper wires strung between poles carried the signals from coast to coast . . . but no farther because it was impossible to build poles in the sea.

This problem was solved in 1850 with the development of a waterproof cable. The first one linked Great Britain with neighboring France, and 16 years later the world's biggest steamship, *Great Eastern*, unreeled a cable to link Europe and the U.S. By 1880 lines stretched around the world. Morse's dream of worldwide "instantaneous communication" had come true.

Telephone

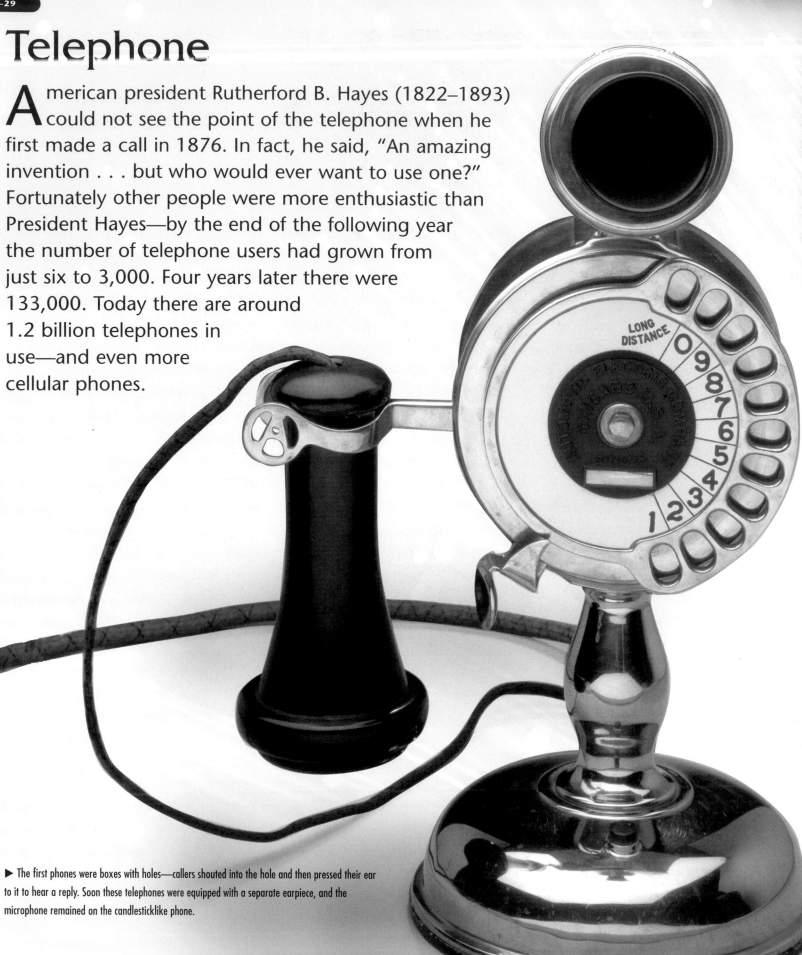

American president Rutherford B. Hayes (1822–1893) could not see the point of the telephone when he first made a call in 1876. In fact, he said, "An amazing invention . . . but who would ever want to use one?" Fortunately other people were more enthusiastic than President Hayes—by the end of the following year the number of telephone users had grown from just six to 3,000. Four years later there were 133,000. Today there are around 1.2 billion telephones in use—and even more cellular phones.

▶ The first phones were boxes with holes—callers shouted into the hole and then pressed their ear to it to hear a reply. Soon these telephones were equipped with a separate earpiece, and the microphone remained on the candlesticklike phone.

Inventive immigrants

One American immigrant built the first working telephone, and another made the phone system a success. In 1849 Italian-American Antonio Meucci (1808–1896) was using electricity to treat a headache when he discovered a way to send speech across the wires. He died before he could develop the telephone, and it was left to the Scottish-American Alexander Graham Bell (1847–1922) to perfect the device in 1876.

Phones may have been new, but the telephone network was not. Calls traveled down telegraph lines that had grown like a spiderweb across the world over the previous 20 years.

Ask the operator

The first phones connected to these lines had no dials. Callers asked an operator for the number they wanted. This changed in 1891 when Almon

Strowger (1839–1902) invented the automatic telephone exchange. He devised the exchange because his funeral business was not making very much money. He guessed that when people called the operator and asked for "an undertaker," she was connecting the call to a rival. His automatic exchange solved the problem, allowing people to just dial the number that they wanted. Because most telephone operators were women, he called his invention the "girlless, curseless, out-of-orderless, waitless telephone."

Clicking switches

The undertaker's invention worked so well that it was used almost unchanged for 70 years. The world of telephones had moved on a long way by the time electronic exchanges eplaced Almon Strowger's clicking switches. In 1978 trials began of a radical new type of telephone—the cellular phone. Previously cellular phones, or cell phones, were expensive and hard to find because each one used a separate radio channel—and there were very few free channels. New phones use computer technology to allow many cell phones to share fewer radio channels without interference.

Luxury phones

Often we take for granted our ability to talk to friends at the push of a button. But what is essential to us is an impossible luxury for many—half of the people in the world cannot afford a phone and have never made a phone call.

▼ Radio beacons for cell phone calls communicate with just a few phones in a "cell"—an area around the beacon.

▶ Today's cell phones have changed the way we communicate in ways that nobody could have guessed. Text messaging, for example, is a surprise success, creating a shorter, quicker way of writing brief messages.

SUMMARY OF CHAPTER 2: FROM ME TO YOU

A to Z of communication

The invention of the alphabet was a breakthrough in personal communication. Alphabets had one sign for each sound used in speech, so learning to write meant learning fewer than 30 letters. The Phoenicians were probably the first people to use an alphabet in the 1000s B.C. The idea was copied by the Greeks and then later by the Romans, who devised the alphabet we use today.

Alphabets did little to speed up long-distance communication—messengers carried notes and letters on foot or on horseback. The great civilizations of Egypt, Rome, and China all had official messenger services to deliver government communications. Private messenger services only began to thrive with the growth of business in 13th-century Europe. Public postal services appeared 200 years later in France and in England. At first only the rich could afford them, but they became more popular with the invention of a prepaid letter delivered anywhere for the same low price.

Speeding up the signal

For simple messages there were some quick alternatives to sending letters. Smoke or fire beacons helped people communicate almost immediately over short distances. By flashing sunlight off of mirrors or flying flags, it became possible to send longer signals. A French inventor devised a chain of telegraph towers with flapping arms to keep the entire country in touch.

The electric telegraph replaced the semaphore signaling system in the mid-1800s. The most successful telegraph was named after the American painter Samuel Morse. It was Morse who pioneered the network of wires and the dot-and-dash electrical pulses that flowed through them.

Speech began to travel through the same wires with the invention of the telephone around 1870. All calls were connected by operators until an automatic exchange-and-dial telephone was invented. This system remained in use for 70 years. As it stopped being used in the 1970s, a new type of telephone was being developed. Using radio waves instead of wires, it became the cellular telephone network that today rivals home phones, or landlines.

Go further . . .

View an alphabet history:
www.ancientscripts.com/
alphabet.html

Learn how communication technologies have grown from the telegraph to broadband:
www.connected-earth.com

Use the semaphore signaling system:
www.anbg.gov.au/flags/semaphore

The Victorian Internet, The Remarkable Story of the Telegraph, and The Nineteenth Century's Online Pioneers
by Tom Standage
(Berkley Pub. Group, 1999)

The Story of Thomas Alva Edison
by Margaret Cousins
(Random House, 1997)

Courier
Delivers urgent documents and packages by bicycle or motorcylce.

Network engineer
Uses knowledge of computer science and electrical and electronic engineering to design communication networks for voice and data.

Mail sorting technician
Installs and maintains sorting and processing equipment in mail centers.

Customer support adviser
Deals with customer and staff problems at a telephone company.

Visit Antonio Meucci's house:
Garibaldi-Meucci Museum
420 Tompkins Avenue
Staten Island, NY 10305
Phone: (718) 442-1608
www.garibaldimeuccimuseum.org

Explore the history of Great Britain's mail service:
Bath Postal Museum
Bath, England BA1 5JL
Phone: 44 1225 460333
www.bathpostalmuseum.org

See how Denmark's mail and telephone services grew:
Danish Post and Telephone Museum
1012 Copenhagen, Denmark
Phone: 45 33 41 09 00

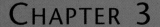

CHAPTER 3

Spreading the word

Pages of white paper, tiny metal letters, and sticky ink hardly seem like materials that could change the world. Yet when Johannes Gutenberg (c. 1400–1468) first brought them together, that is exactly what happened. Communication was no longer personal, and ideas and knowledge quickly spread. Although printing remained the most powerful way of communicating for around 400 years, in the 1800s and 1900s rivals appeared. Photography made lifelike copies of what we see and then printed them. Movies brought these still pictures to life. Recorded sound did for our ears what photography had done for our eyes, and radio transmitters sent speech and music all around the world. Television has had an effect that has been almost as dramatic as printing. In many countries this bright and noisy box is the main source of news and entertainment.

Printing

Imagine copying an entire book by writing every word with a pen. It seems like an impossible task, but all books were once made this way. The introduction of printing around 1440 put scribes out of work. In the time it took a scribe to write one expensive book, a printer could make one thousand cheap ones. The new, printed books gave poorer people something to read, and the books spread radical new ideas that challenged the world of religion and science.

▲ Long before Gutenberg, pictures had been printed using blocks of wood carved with an image in reverse. Inking them and pressing them onto paper transferred the picture. However, carving words on a wood block was even slower than writing them by hand.

▲ Movable type only had one letter on it. After one page had been printed the letters could be taken apart and rearranged to print the next page.

Printing pioneer

The German goldsmith Johannes Gutenberg (c. 1400–1468) was responsible for this huge change in written communication. Around 1440 he started to make movable type—tiny lead blocks, each one with one raised letter on top. Arranged to form sentences and rolled with ink, the type transferred the text onto paper that was pressed against it.

◀ Although Gutenberg's books were cheaper than hand-written ones, they still cost a worker three years' salary. However, they did not make Gutenberg rich—in 1455 he failed to pay off a loan and went out of business.

▲ Alois Senefelder used a smooth block of limestone to print. Today's presses use printing plates instead. Curved around a drum, the plate turns constantly, pressing words and pictures onto the paper that passes under it.

Gutenberg did not actually invent printing—or the type, ink, or paper. Simple printing from engraved seals began in China 2,700 years earlier, and a Chinese printer, Pi Cheng, made movable type out of pottery 400 years before Gutenberg. However, Gutenberg *did* have one great idea: he took a press used for smoothing out bedsheets and squeezed the paper and inky type together.

A revolution in knowledge

Gutenberg's idea had far-reaching effects. The following century printed books spread the ideas of religious thinker Martin Luther (1483–1546). His challenge to the power of the pope split Christians into Protestants and Catholics. Printing also overturned long-held scientific beliefs such as the idea that the universe turns around Earth. When Italian scientist Galileo Galilei (1564–1642) proved instead that Earth orbits the Sun, he spread the news in a printed book.

Printing with wax and water

Movable type was the most common way to print until the end of the 1700s. In 1796 Alois Senefelder (1771–1834) used a wax crayon to write a laundry list on a slab of polished stone. He found that if he dampened the stone, ink from a roller would only stick to the waxy writing. Pressing paper onto the inky stone copied the text.

Giant presses

Today most printing works by Senefelder's method, called lithography. Instead of printing on single sheets of paper, the biggest presses now print on huge paper rolls. They print in color by using a regular pattern of tiny dots colored yellow, cyan (blue), magenta (pink), and black. Too small to see without a magnifying glass, the dots merge together to give the impression of a full-color picture.

Digital or paper?

Ink on paper may seem old-fashioned in an age when the Internet provides lightning-quick access to seemingly unlimited information. However, books, newspapers, and magazines will be with us for a long time to come. After all, they do not need battery power, and you can read them anywhere. You can write on the pages—and unlike computers, they never crash!

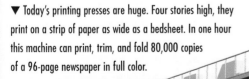

▼ Today's printing presses are huge. Four stories high, they print on a strip of paper as wide as a bedsheet. In one hour this machine can print, trim, and fold 80,000 copies of a 96-page newspaper in full color.

The printed word

When printing began in Germany, there were only a few thousand books in all of Europe. However, just 50 years later printers had produced more than nine million copies. At first they sold the books themselves, but as numbers and demand grew, a new business—publishing—began. Publishers organized the production and sale of books, newspapers, and magazines, but they never got their fingers inky. Printers were paid to set the type, operate the printing press, and bind the finished books.

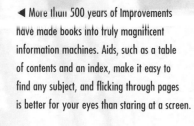

◀ More than 500 years of Improvements have made books into truly magnificent information machines. Aids, such as a table of contents and an index, make it easy to find any subject, and flicking through pages is better for your eyes than staring at a screen.

First books

The first printed matter was religious. Gutenberg started printing indulgences—slips of paper that people bought to reduce the time they would spend in hell when they died. He then moved on to Bibles and prayer books. However, it was not long before printers branched out into encyclopedias, schoolbooks, and other general reference books—one of the first books published in England was called *The game and playe of the Chesse.*

Pamphlets to newsletters

It was a long time before printers used their presses to report news. When they did, it was usually to spread the word about an event such as a famous battle. From the start of the 1500s they printed eyewitnesses' accounts in the form of pamphlets. Bankers also made newsletters for their customers. As well as business information, they printed general news.

Newspapers spread

The bankers' publications only came out occasionally. Real newspapers that appeared regularly began circulating around 100 years later. The first was probably the monthly *Relation of Select and Noteworthy Happenings* published in Strasbourg, Germany, in 1609. Other publishers in Germany and the Netherlands quickly copied the idea. However, the newspaper was slower to spread beyond Europe. Even in 1866 an international traveler from Japan to Europe had to explain to his friends back home what a newspaper was. He told them that from it a reader could learn about current events ". . . though he remains indoors and does not see what goes on outside."

Today newspapers and books are published just about everywhere. Worldwide, 84,000 newspapers are published daily, and around 550 million people read them. There is just as much variety in books and magazines—850,000 new book titles are published every year.

▼ Putting a daily newspaper together is a stressful job. Editors and designers only have a few hours to organize pictures and stories from around the corner and from around the world. The newspaper has to be printed overnight so that it is ready to be on newsstands by dawn.

Comics and cartoons

The first thing that many people do when they open the newspaper is turn to the comics. Amusing drawings are almost 500 years old, but comic strips only began in 1896 with the publication of *The Yellow Kid* in a New York newspaper. The story of this poor child was aimed at adults, and it boosted the paper's sales. This is still true today—the best comics entertain everyone, and—as "graphic novels"—comics are bought and read by both children and serious collectors.

Publishing people

Putting together a newspaper or magazine takes an incredible amount of work. Journalists, photographers, and illustrators provide the raw material, and experts at publishing companies prepare it for printing. Editors choose what will be included, and graphic designers decide what the pages will look like. They work with picture researchers who find photographs and illustrations in picture libraries. Finally production staff gather everything together and send it to the printers.

◀ When recording a live performance, sound engineers usually aim for the most accurate copy of what the audience hears. By routing the signals from each microphone and instrument pickup to a separate recording track, they can adjust and balance the overall sound later.

Recording sound

Soaring guitar riffs and pounding bass throb from today's tiny MP3 players. Although this digital technology is changing how we buy and use recorded sound, it has not eliminated vinyl. The shiny, black plastic discs that still dominate the dance floor have a surprisingly long history. They first appeared in 1888 and spun almost unchanged for more than 100 years. Recorded sound itself is even older. It began in the laboratory of Thomas Edison.

The machine that spoke
Edison (1847–1931) had the idea of recording sound in the summer of 1877. The "talking machine" that he sketched had a cylinder covered in tinfoil with a crank to turn it. His engineer built the machine, and to everyone's surprise it worked the first time. By turning the cylinder while shouting into a funnel, Edison indented the tinfoil with a wiggly groove. Each wiggle copied the pulses of air pressure that make up sounds. In order to play back the sound, he used another needle that followed the grooves, amplifying its movements with a stretched paper disc. Edison never dreamed his simple invention would

► For some people, digital sound will never replace vinyl. Disc jockeys like the control they have over vinyl discs and the possibilities they offer for mixing and scratching. Music lovers prefer vinyl because they believe that CDs produce inferior sound quality.

amount to much, describing it as "a mere toy." He was almost right. Although, at first, his phonograph astonished the public, the novelty wore off quickly.

The first discs

What turned sound recording from a toy into a way of playing and selling music was an invention that came ten years later. German-American Émile Berliner (1851–1925) replaced Edison's cylinders with flat discs. They were more compact and did not wear out as quickly as cylinders. But most importantly they were easy to make. From a metal "master" disc Berliner could press thousands of identical copies.

Magnetic sound

Like Edison's system, Berliner's players were mechanical—they did not use electricity. Electrical recording began when Danish engineer Valdemar Poulsen (1869–1942) invented his telegraphone in 1898. This stored sound in a reel of iron wire, magnetized in a pattern that copied the pulses of speech and music.

Digital music

Poulsen's invention was mostly used as a telephone answering machine and hardly affected recorded music at first. Berliner's discs continued to be the most common way of playing music at home until the introduction of the compact disc (CD) by the Sony and Phillips corporations in 1983. These discs stored music digitally—as computer data—eliminating the clicks and pops of vinyl.

CDs are still a favorite way of playing music, but even this is changing fast. A quiet revolution in music started in 1989 when Germany's Fraunhofer Institute found a way to make music data files ten times smaller. As MP3s, songs are easy to trade on the Internet and download onto pocket-sized electronic jukeboxes. Soon MP3s may make CDs look as old-fashioned as Edison's cylinders.

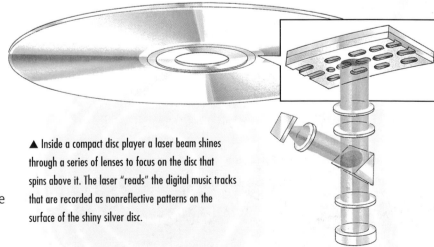

▲ Inside a compact disc player a laser beam shines through a series of lenses to focus on the disc that spins above it. The laser "reads" the digital music tracks that are recorded as nonreflective patterns on the surface of the shiny silver disc.

▲ Daguerre used a camera like this one—so did William Fox Talbot (1800–1877), an Englishman who invented a different photographic process independent from Daguerre.

▲ A modern digital camera is a tiny computer with a lens. A light-sensitive silicon chip inside the camera captures images, shows them on the tiny screen, and saves them onto a memory card.

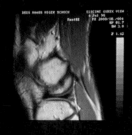

▲ Medical instruments that look inside the body make pictures that are similar to photographs. These images, created using computerized axial tomography (CAT) scanning, help doctors detect tumors.

Photography

It is hard to imagine a world without photography. Maybe we could give up snapshots, but magazines would look boring if drawings and paintings were their only images. Photography is not only used for entertainment but also for communication. Special cameras etch the patterns on silicon chips used in computers and television—equipment vital for communication. In hospitals doctors would have to live without X-rays and CAT scans because both of these use types of photography.

The first photographer

In the first week of January 1839 French scene painter Louis Daguerre (1789–1851) suddenly became one of the most famous men in Paris, France. Daguerre had invented a mirror with a memory. He had found a way to make shiny silver plates record perfect, lifelike pictures inside a camera. Fellow French artists were astonished and alarmed, and one artist said "from today painting is dead!" Before Daguerre's invention the only way to create a picture was with a brush or a pencil—and a lot of of skill.

Color and movement

In fact, artists had nothing to be afraid of. Daguerre could only photograph objects that were perfectly still—even the leaves on trees were blurred,

Although modern cameras are easy to use, taking photographs for magazines, newspapers, and advertisements still requires skill and a lot of training. Here the photographer is using elaborate lighting to shoot a fashion advertisement, with help from an assistant and a hairstylist.

and portraits were impossible. The "Daguerrotypes," as the shiny pictures were called, were in black and white. However, improvements to photography gradually removed these obstacles, and by 1877 it was possible to take a photograph of a galloping horse. Color photography took another 30 years to perfect.

Snapshots!

For a long time taking pictures meant buying a lot of expensive equipment. Photographers developed and printed their own pictures in darkrooms—special rooms that do not let in light. Then in 1888 the American inventor George Eastman (1854–1932) began to sell box-shaped cameras made out of cardboard. With the slogan "You press the button, we do the rest," Eastman made photography trouble free. His cardboard "Kodaks" were just like today's disposable cameras. When the film was finished, you sent the whole camera back to the maker, who printed the pictures.

Photography now

This clever idea meant that you did not have to be an expert in order to take good pictures. Eastman started the snapshot industry that today allows us to capture and share pictures of happy moments. Although photography began with a camera, lens, light, and film, in order to take good photographs today you do not need all of these things.

Digital cameras and many scientific image-making instruments use electronic sensors instead of film. And by replacing light with magnetic fields, infrared beams, or X-rays, we can see deep inside the human body—and look at the farthest corners of the universe.

These special uses of photography expand our knowledge and help save lives. However, the main value of the camera is still in communication and entertainment. Despite the advance of television and cinema, images in newspapers and magazines still have greater power to anger, shock, and amuse us. By capturing a moment in time, photography gives us a unique view of the world that moving pictures can never really match.

◄ In *Harry Potter and The Chamber of Secrets* computer graphics give Harry Potter extra help when he misses the Hogwarts Express. But when the flying car realistically swoops through the arches of the viaduct, it is hard not to believe in magic.

Cinema

▼ Putting a coin into one of Thomas Edison's kinetoscopes showed a 20-second-long movie that only one person could watch at a time. The American inventor thought that projected movies were no threat to his one-at-a-time movies. Foolishly he refused to project his films, saying, "If we make this screen machine, it will spoil everything."

W hen cars fly through the air or an action hero seems about to die, we know that what we are watching on the movie screen is not real. But the magic of movies is so powerful that we all gasp and sit on the edges of our seats, our hearts pounding with excitement. This ability to thrill, surprise, and terrify audiences has helped keep movie theaters full ever since motion pictures first hit the big screen in 1895.

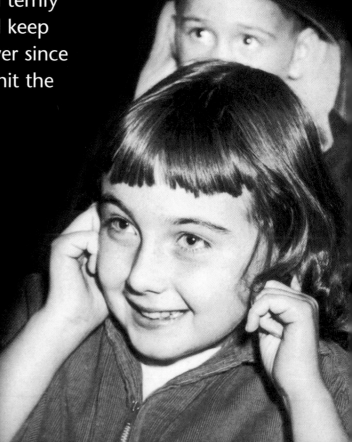

► Movies are one of the most powerful ways of communicating. The darkness, the huge screen, and the loud, surround-sound block out all other thoughts and senses. No wonder we cover our eyes at the scary scenes!

Moving picture toys
Motion pictures did not begin with the first movies. More than 150 years earlier scientists had shown that if we flick quickly enough through a series of slightly different drawings, we do not see any one individual picture clearly. Instead the pictures move as if they are alive.

Not exactly a movie
The invention of photography (see page 38) made this trick even more real. In 1878 England's Eadweard Muybridge (1830–1904) used 12 cameras to take a dozen photographs of a speeding horse in just half a second. Flashed quickly in front of viewers, the horse galloped realistically. Although Muybridge's invention was limited to a couple of seconds of movement, he inspired inventors, and they looked for ways to show longer sequences.

Film on a loop
The first inventor to have any real success was William Dickson (1860–1935), who worked in the laboratory of Thomas Edison. Dickson built a camera that could take an endless series of photographs on a roll of film and show them in rapid sequence in order to recreate movement. Edison told Dickson what to do and then patented the system himself as the "kinetoscope."

Screen machine
Although the kinetoscope showed real movies, it was the work of two French brothers that turned movies into an art form. Auguste (1862–1954) and Louis Lumière (1864–1948) had the clever idea of projecting movies onto a screen in a darkened room so that many people could watch the movie together. At one of their first movie viewings in 1895 they showed an express train rushing toward the camera. Some members of the audience were so terrified that they ran for the exit!

Sound and color
The Lumière brothers' movies—and the thousands that followed them—were not only black-and-white, but they were also silent. Printed text appeared onscreen to explain what people were saying, and a pianist or orchestra provided musical accompaniment. The first movies with sound appeared in 1900, and true-color movies were only made 17 years later.

Although the invention of television and video cut movie audiences, people still line up to see the latest blockbusters on the big screen. It is easy to see why movie theaters remain full—TV just cannot compete with the experience of watching movies on a giant screen and sharing the thrills, excitement, and tears with hundreds of other movie fans.

◀ Using studios, outside broadcast units, and recordings, radio stations mix news, music, sports, discussion, drama, and entertainment. Taxes pay for public service stations, and advertising (see page 58) covers the cost of broadcasts from other stations.

Radio

Think of radio, and you probably think of a boombox blaring out music on the beach. But radio does much more than just entertain us. Tiny radio chips cordlessly connect our portable telephone calls and computer printers. Radio waves are used to send distress signals from sinking ships, to communicate with spacecraft, and to navigate on land, at sea, and in the air. In fact, without radio we would literally be lost!

◀ Radio was first used by crews onboard ships to communicate with each other. But when the *Titanic* sank in 1912, other ships overlooked the distress signals broadcast by her radio operator (played here by an actor), and around 1,500 people drowned. After the *Titanic* disaster laws were passed that forced all ships to keep their radios on day and night.

Guglielmo Marconi

The man who made modern-day radio possible was an Italian student, Guglielmo Marconi (1874–1937). Marconi realized that radio waves could be used to replace telegraph wires (see page 26) and began experimenting at home in 1894. Using very simple equipment, he managed to send a radio signal across a room and then to the end of his yard. Next his brother carried a homemade radio receiver out of sight to the neighboring valley. When he received Guglielmo's signals, he replied by firing a hunting gun up into the air!

Long-distance signals

Marconi's invention was called "wireless telegraphy" because it sent Morse code messages without the wires that connected telegraph stations. Wireless telegraphy seemed a useful way to communicate with ships, but unfortunately Guglielmo could not interest anyone in Italy in his work. So he traveled to England to develop his idea. There he signaled over longer and longer distances—across London, across a flat plain, and across the sea. Triumphantly in 1901 he sent a signal across the Atlantic Ocean.

▶ Radio waves have different frequencies (channels), and each one carries a different radio station. So by tuning in a radio, we can listen to many different stations. And unlike most entertainment, we do not have to pay anything for it.

Words and music

Marconi's "wireless" sent only Morse code. But radio became more interesting in 1906 when U.S. inventor Reginald Fessenden (1866–1932) transmitted speech and music. His signals surprised radio operators on nearby ships, who had only ever heard the crackle of dots and dashes in their headphones.

Fessenden's breakthrough made the radio broadcasts that we take for granted possible. Early radio signals usually connected two individual stations, allowing them to exchange messages. But radio broadcasts were different. A single radio station sent out the signals, while hundreds, thousands, or even millions of

people with radio receivers listened in. Regular broadcasts began in the U.S. around 1920, and KDKA in Pittsburgh was one of the first radio stations on the air.

Digital future

Today radio waves help us in so many ways that we hardly even realize that we are using them. Following the invention of integrated circuits (silicon chips) around 1960, radio sets became smaller and cheaper. Computers and digital technology enabled engineers to make even better use of radio. And in a twist that might make Marconi laugh, today's digital radio is broadcast as a series of on-off pulses—much like his original Morse code signals.

▶ Unlike waves in water or sound waves in air, radio waves do not need a material to travel through. This allows broadcasts from Earth to reach out into space, enabling us to keep in touch with astronauts such as Dr. Mamoru Mohri during Mission STS-47 in 1992.

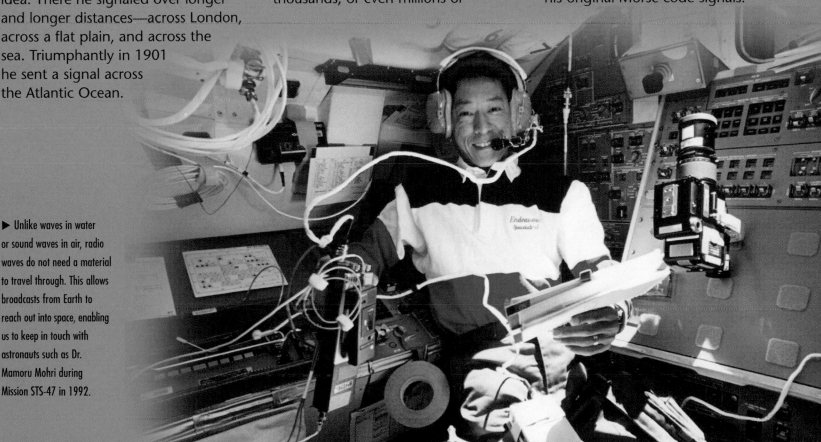

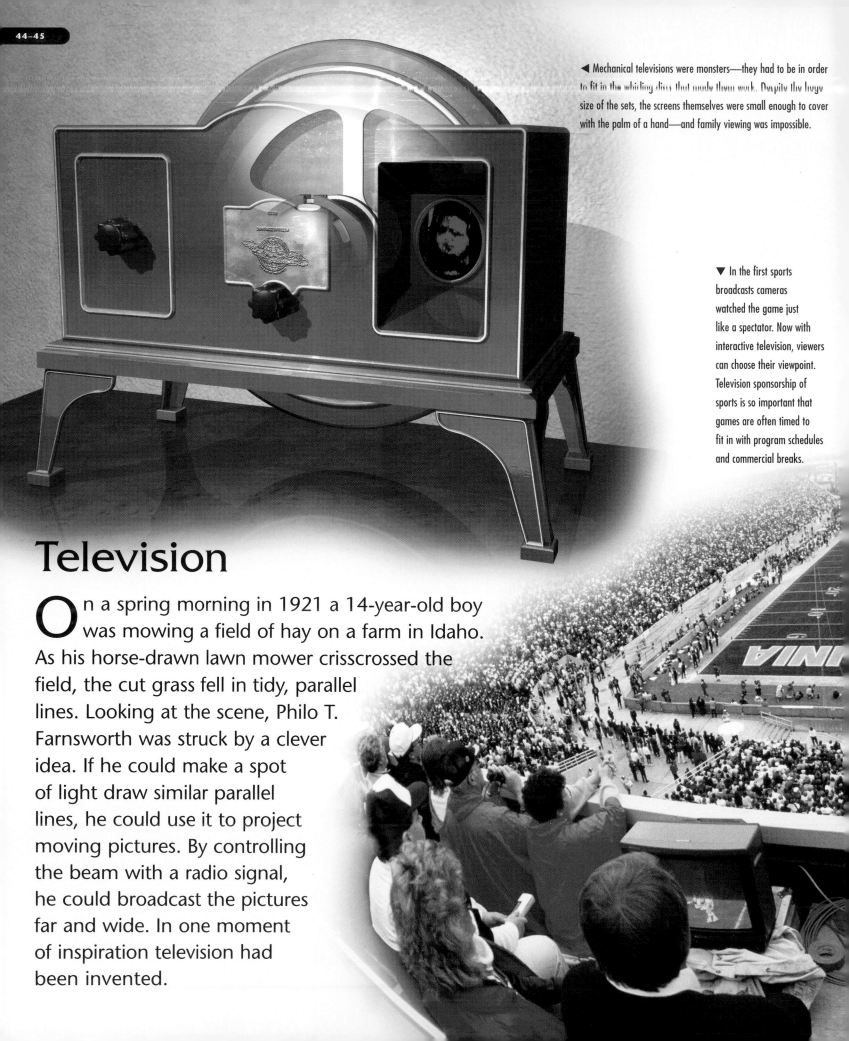

◀ Mechanical televisions were monsters—they had to be in order to fit in the whirling discs that made them work. Despite the huge size of the sets, the screens themselves were small enough to cover with the palm of a hand—and family viewing was impossible.

▼ In the first sports broadcasts cameras watched the game just like a spectator. Now with interactive television, viewers can choose their viewpoint. Television sponsorship of sports is so important that games are often timed to fit in with program schedules and commercial breaks.

Television

On a spring morning in 1921 a 14-year-old boy was mowing a field of hay on a farm in Idaho. As his horse-drawn lawn mower crisscrossed the field, the cut grass fell in tidy, parallel lines. Looking at the scene, Philo T. Farnsworth was struck by a clever idea. If he could make a spot of light draw similar parallel lines, he could use it to project moving pictures. By controlling the beam with a radio signal, he could broadcast the pictures far and wide. In one moment of inspiration television had been invented.

Hay field into TV set

Turning his bright idea into a television set was not going to be easy, but Farnsworth was smart—and determined. He raised enough money to do some basic experiments, and by the time he was 20 he had managed to produce a simple electronic television image. At the time most television sets used motors and whirling discs in order to produce images. Farnsworth's invention had no moving parts. It was simpler, more reliable—and he was sure it would soon produce much better pictures.

Powerful rivals

Philo was confident of success, but he had powerful rivals. The giant radio company RCA offered to buy his invention. When he would not sell, they perfected their own system with the help of a Russian-born radio engineer named Vladimir Zworykin. RCA could not avoid using some of Farnsworth's ideas and was forced to pay him for them. Nevertheless, the inventor felt he had been cheated of the fame and fortune that he deserved. By the age of 33 he was depressed and forgotten. In contrast, his invention flourished. Electronic TV sets of the type that Farnsworth pioneered began to receive programs all over the world.

▲ As anyone who has "channel surfed" on cable or satellite knows, more channels does not always mean better viewing because good television programs are expensive to produce. Although this technician at a television station monitors up to 90 channels, many show programs of little interest to most viewers.

The colorful 50s

These first television programs were in black and white. Research on color television had begun in the 1930s, but it was a long time before the pictures were as clear as on black-and-white television sets. Color broadcasts began in the U.S. in 1951, but only around two dozen people had television sets that could receive them. It was not until 1971 that sales of color television sets overtook those of black-and-white sets.

Television today

The television sets we watch our favorite shows on today are much bigger and brighter than those from the 1970s. However, the biggest change has been in what we watch, not in how we watch it. Satellite and cable television allow us to see a huge variety of shows about all types of special interests and hobbies. Equally as important, cable technology also allows television companies to broadcast shows to just one town—and to provide its citizens with their own channel and regional news.

Now with digital video cameras (see page 46) and a little training and practice, anyone can make and show a television program. Sit and watch TV for long enough, and sooner or later you will see your friends, your town— maybe even yourself—on-screen!

Video and DVD

Television has become such an important part of our lives that the familiar faces we see on the screen feel like friends. Even better, with a video cassette recorder (VCR) or digital versatile disc (DVD) player, we can meet up with them at any time. However, it was not always like this— before video people had to rush home to watch their favorite shows. Video has affected television in another important way—with a video camera, or camcorder, we can go beyond the television set and create our own shows. With digital video, we can use a home computer to make them almost as polished as a Hollywood movie.

And now, on tape . . .

Today live television shows are rare, but until the 1950s all television shows were broadcast exactly as they happened. This caused problems for broadcasters in the U.S. Because of the different time zones, viewers in New York City would have to stay awake until midnight to watch a sports event played at 9 P.M. in Los Angeles, California. In 1956 engineers at the U.S. Ampex Corporation changed this when they found a way to record television images and sound onto magnetic tape. The tape was as wide as a credit card and was wound between two huge, open spools. These recorders were so large and expensive that only the biggest television companies could afford them.

Convenient cassettes

Home video recording started 20 years later with the launch of the "video home system" (VHS) by the giant Japanese electronics company Matsushita. They produced plastic videocassettes, or videotapes, that enclosed spools of narrower tape. Putting a tape into the VCR and pressing the record button triggered the machine to pull the tape out and to lace it around the drum that recorded and played back the television signal.

▶ Home video has changed the way that we remember the past. Memories may fade, but in the red, green, and blue lines of a television picture a video shows us for what we are— in our true colors—five, ten, or 20 years later.

Time shifting

The first VCRs were expensive, but the price quickly fell, and they became popular as a way of watching prerecorded movies. Viewers also used VCRs for "time shifting"—recording shows in order to watch them at a more convenient time. Today DVDs are replacing videotapes for watching the latest blockbusters. Although they look similar to compact discs (CDs), DVDs hold much more information—in addition to a movie, a DVD may also contain previews, games, or even a soundtrack in another language.

Lights . . . camera . . . ACTION!

If VCRs changed the way we watch TV, then camcorders did something even more important. They changed how we see and remember ourselves and our families. Home movies were hardly new when camcorders appeared, but shooting a home movie was slow and expensive. Cameras only held four minutes of film, which needed processing before you could set up a projector, darken the room, and watch it. Video, by comparison, provided instant replay on an ordinary TV.

The dawn of digital

Early video cameras were big and heavy and were linked to a separate recorder by a thick cable. One-piece "camcorders" appeared in 1982. The newest camcorders store images and sound digitally. They are tiny and accessible, but more importantly they make video editing simple. By copying a video onto a computer, you can cut out mistakes and dull shots and add music, sound effects, and titles. Carefully "cutting" a video can turn it from a two-hour yawn into an action-packed, 20-minute, real-life drama!

▶ Using computer software, such as Apple's iMovie, you can change the order of video shots, fade between them, and add new scenes shot later in different places. When your editing is done, you can burn the finished movie onto a DVD.

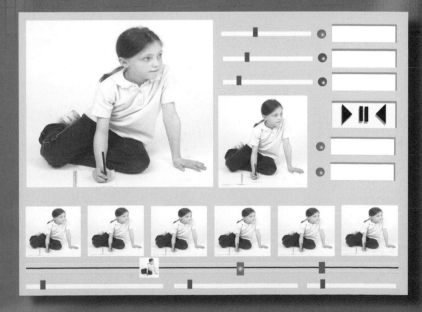

SUMMARY OF CHAPTER 3: SPREADING THE WORD

A new way of putting words on paper

Until the invention of the printing press writing was the only way to copy and spread information. The press led to an explosion of knowledge, and printers developed the book into a form that was useful for both reference and entertainment. Although printing methods have improved, books themselves have hardly changed at all.

At first the printers sold the books they made, but with time publishers began to organize book production. They paid the author and printer and then sold the books to stores. Publishers also made pamphlets, newspapers, and magazines. Together these printed communications reached millions of people.

New ways of multiplying information did not appear until the 1800s. The camera spread pictures as efficiently as the printing press spread words. Developed around 160 years ago, at first photography captured only completely still subjects in shades of gray. Action photography had to wait 30 years and color photography, 60 years.

Inventing a talking machine

Sound recording was the idea of Thomas Edison, but his 1877 cylinder recorder was a toy. Discs invented ten years later made sound recording popular—they were not replaced with today's digital CDs until the 1980s. It was also Edison who pioneered moving pictures with a coin-operated viewer. Projected movies first showed the images on the big screen in 1895, with sound following soon after.

We owe the discovery of radio to Guglielmo Marconi. Marconi could not interest anyone in the wireless telegraph in his native country, Italy, so he took it to Great Britain. There he sent signals over long distances, and in 1901 the signals crossed the Atlantic Ocean. Five years later the transmission of speech and music made the news and entertainment broadcasts we enjoy today possible.

Transmitting pictures was a dream until the 1920s, when mechanical television was invented. Its spinning disc made tiny pictures, but with the development of electronic television, it was quickly forgotten. With the addition of color and videotape recording, television has become the most powerful communication tool yet invented.

Go further . . .

View an animated history of books:
www.bbc.co.uk/arts/books/historyofbooks

See how people took photographs 150 years ago:
www.nmpft.org.uk/insight/onexhib_photoequip.asp

Read about the early days of motion pictures:
www.americanhistory.si.edu/cinema

Find out how the British Broadcasting Corporation (BBC) transmitted its first radio program:
www.sciencemuseum.org.uk/exhibitions/2lo

Book editor
Plans and coordinates printed books in collaboration with authors, illustrators, and designers and then checks and corrects the text.

Journalist
Collects news and other stories for broadcast media such as television, newspapers, and magazines.

Photographic assistant
Helps run a photographic studio, assisting the photographer during all aspects of a shoot.

Sound recording engineer
Transfers an artist's performance to tape and helps mix the sound to a finished recording, ready for release.

Visit the house where Thomas Edison was born:
9 Edison Drive
Milan, OH 44846
Phone: (419) 499-2135
www.tomedison.org

Produce a radio show:
The Science Museum
London, England SW7 2DD
Phone: 44 870 870 4868
www.sciencemuseum.org.uk/galleryguide/E3040.asp

See a recreation of Gutenberg's printing press in his hometown:
Gutenberg Museum
Rhineland-Palatinate, Germany
Phone: 49 6131 232 955

CHAPTER 4

The global village

The term "global village" was first used to describe a world wired for instant communication. In a global village talking to someone on the other side of the world would be easy—as if the globe had shrunk to the size of a village. In this chapter you can trace the progress of the technologies, such as satellites and the Internet, that made the global village a reality.

As communication has become more widespread, the urge to control it has also increased. The Internet makes this difficult. Distributed around the world in a million computers, it is everywhere but at the same time nowhere definite. If one computer is switched off, messages and Web pages flow another way to their destination. This self-healing ability makes the World Wide Web open and free for all. However, openness is not always an advantage. You can never be sure whether your messages are safe. This is an age-old problem, and the speed of communication has made it more important than ever.

Satellites

Look up at the sky at dusk or dawn, and you might see a bright speck quickly move across it. It is not a star or a comet—it is a satellite orbiting Earth. Satellites like these are essential links in communication networks—they relay telephone calls, broadcast TV shows, and provide Internet connections. The satellites you can see are in low earth orbit—around 50 mi. (80km) up. However, most communications satellites circle much higher than this, and they orbit at the same speed that Earth turns, so they look like they are hovering in a fixed spot above the equator.

▼ Powered by unfolding solar panels, communication satellites are like orbiting radio stations, relaying microwave signals between ground stations on opposite sides of the globe. Earth's gravity keeps them trapped in orbit, stopping them from spinning off into space.

▼ Satellite telephones can be a money-saving way of providing a basic telephone service in out-of-the-way places. Although it is expensive, a satellite telephone service could be cheaper than running cables.

Not a bad idea

Called "geostationary satellites," these orbiting craft were the idea of science fiction writer Arthur C. Clarke (born 1917). In 1945 he suggested launching satellites up to exactly 22,258 mi. (35,900km), where they would orbit Earth only once per day. From there they could receive radio signals broadcast from a base station on Earth and retransmit them to another distant spot on the ground.

At the time people made fun of Clarke because satellites had never been launched. But Clarke had the last laugh. Within 20 years a satellite called *Early Bird* began relaying telephone calls and television pictures exactly as he had predicted.

A new way of talking

Satellites quickly changed the way we communicate. Within 15 years they carried more than two thirds

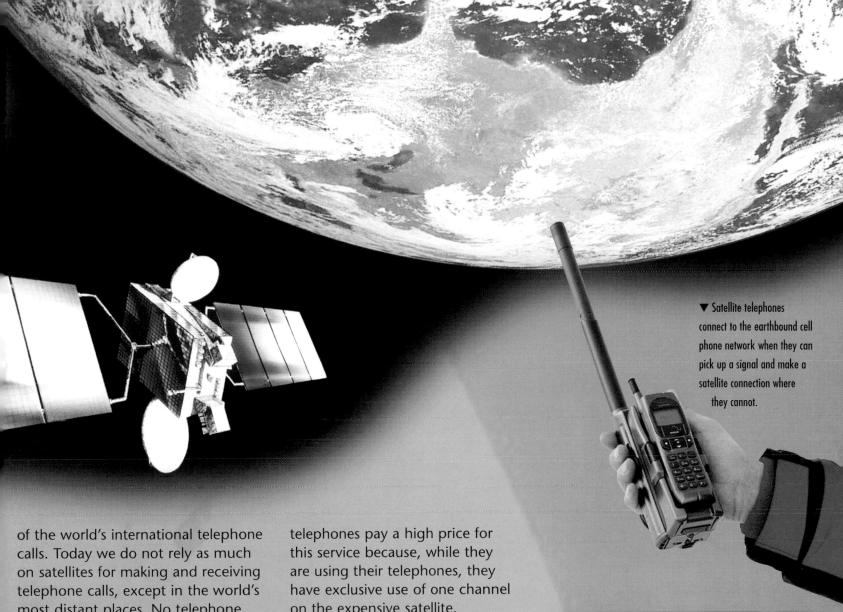

▼ Satellite telephones connect to the earthbound cell phone network when they can pick up a signal and make a satellite connection where they cannot.

of the world's international telephone calls. Today we do not rely as much on satellites for making and receiving telephone calls, except in the world's most distant places. No telephone cables reach these remote areas, and they are out of range of the beacons that provide cellular telephone coverage (see page 28). Satellites fill this gap, allowing explorers and soldiers to call home.

"Sorry to keep you waiting . . ."

The satellite telephones that use geostationary satellites need to be extremely powerful because the satellite is so far away. Calls made and received using these telephones also have awkward delays because the signal takes around half a second to reach the satellite and return to Earth. However, a new generation of telephones has overcome these problems by using satellites much closer to Earth. Users of satellite

telephones pay a high price for this service because, while they are using their telephones, they have exclusive use of one channel on the expensive satellite.

Television in orbit

Compared to the cost of satellite telephone calls, satellite television is cheap and readily available. It uses geostationary satellites to beam television signals to small regions of the Earth's surface. Because millions of television viewers receive the same satellite channels, they share the high price of the satellite and broadcasting system, and each viewer pays a relatively small amount for the service.

The first home satellite television systems, introduced in 1983, needed receiving dishes as big as beach umbrellas, but the most modern systems use rooftop dishes not much bigger than a dinner plate.

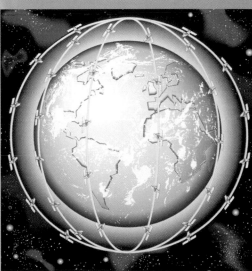

▲ The Iridium phone system uses 66 satellites in low earth orbit. Each satellite circles Earth every 100 minutes. The system eliminates delays in speech, and it is the only way to make telephone calls from the poles and other distant places.

The Internet

Spreading across the globe in a tangled and complicated web, the Internet connects hundreds of millions of computers. The amazing thing about this giant communication network is that, in order to use it, we do not need to know a lot about it. Just clicking a button can connect us to friends across the globe—or around the corner. The Internet's creators never dreamed it would be used to book movie tickets, order take-out food, or play games such as chess. This amazing technology began as a way of protecting the United States from missile attacks.

Missiles and radar

During the 1950s and 1960s the United States and the U.S.S.R. (Russia) threatened each other with missiles of terrifying power—this battle became known as the Cold War. To protect the country, U.S. scientists built radar stations to warn of an attack and rockets to knock Soviet missiles out of the sky. In order to connect the radar to the missile bases, they created a complicated computer network called SAGE. The network was extremely slow—today's modems transfer data 50 times faster—but it worked.

▲ Not only is the Internet a useful source of information, but it is also an endless source of entertainment. Games, such as chess, can be played with friends who are at the same school or on the other side of the world.

▲ Inside huge domes like this one, radar dishes scanned the skies for approaching missiles. The first computer networks linked the radar dishes to the missiles, allowing U.S. army chiefs to counterattack if U.S. cities were threatened.

Making it bulletproof

When engineers improved the original system, they added a clever twist. The network that replaced SAGE was bulletproof. If a missile hit part of the new network, the data automatically found a way around the damage.

In the late 1960s U.S. Department of Defense scientists adapted the system to share research information, creating ARPANET. Large universities and then smaller institutions joined the network. By 1983 what we now call the Internet was almost complete.

The World Wide Web

Using ARPANET was not easy—you had to type in complex commands in order for it to work. This changed in the early 1990s when British scientist Tim Berners-Lee (born 1955) created the first Web browser—finding information became as easy as pointing and clicking. Soon afterward Mark Andreesen (born 1971) adapted Berners-Lee's program to run on both Apple Macintoshes (Macs) and personal computers (PCs), calling it Mosaic.

Lightning-quick messages

A speedy rival to the postal system appeared in 1971 when engineer Ray Tomlinson (born 1941) invented e-mail. Working on ARPANET, he figured out a way for researchers to leave messages on each other's computers. He chose the "@" sign to separate a computer user's address from the name of their network because it "seemed to make sense . . . the user was "at" some other network."

Together, Web browsers and e-mail made the Internet simple and appealing, and the number of Internet users grew rapidly. Each year the Internet doubles in size as people discover that it can be a library, a jukebox, a mail carrier, a movie theater, a supermarket . . . and a thousand other useful or entertaining things.

Merging media

How would you like to be able to store your favorite songs on your watch? Or see live football on your cellular phone? Or even read the newspaper on your refrigerator door? As communications become faster and smarter, devices such as telephones, televisions, personal computers, and fax machines are becoming more and more alike. Many magazines and newspapers now have electronic editions. A single, shiny disc can replace a whole shelf of heavy encyclopedias. The only limit on how we will use communication technologies in the future is our imagination.

▼ Camera telephones have been banned at fashion shows in Paris, France. Some rival designers pretended to make calls, but instead they were actually taking snapshots of the clothes in order to make cheap copies.

Fancy phones

Clever software and shrinking computer chips have blurred the differences between the gadgets that we use to communicate. Not long ago we had to use a camera to take vacation snapshots, a computer to surf the Internet, a cell phone to call friends, and a personal stereo to listen to music. Today the smallest cellular telephones can do all of these things.

Wired telephones are also merging with computers and the Internet. Telecommunication companies are already routing some long-distance calls over the Internet. With a little ingenuity, it is possible to use a computer to talk to friends on the other side of the world—free of charge.

No hi-fi needed

Home entertainment is moving in the same direction. By linking a music system to a home network, you can play MP3s stored on a computer in another room. Listening to the radio online, you can hear local programs from your own country or anywhere in the world.

Printed pages

Newspapers and magazines could merge with the electronic world in unusual ways. Although reading a magazine online is not a new experience, what about a newspaper with images that move? Or a whole magazine printed on a single sheet of paper? Digital paper may soon make these things possible. It feels just like regular paper, but its ink appears and disappears under computer control.

The pros and cons

How useful are these devices and new ways of communicating? There is not much point in owning a telephone that does everything if it cannot do anything well.

Figuring out what is useful and what is not will take some time, but new media are pointing the way. You can subscribe to electronic newspapers that show you only articles on subjects that interest you.

▼ MP3s combine music with the Internet. By downloading individual songs off the Web, you can buy the best and skip the rest.

New video recorders download television schedules and record episodes of your favorite show that you have missed.

▲ Although it is time-consuming jotting down notes on a personal organizer, a paper diary and address book would make a much bigger bulge in your pocket. Speech recognition may eventually create an organizer that takes dictation.

Simple but safe

Some of the most successful ideas are also the simplest. The short messaging service (SMS), or text messaging, was at first a minor feature of cellular telephones. However, this joining of the scribbled note and the telephone has created a tool that many people now rely on. So as technologies move closer together, it may be the smallest things that change communication in the most amazing ways.

▼ Merging television, the Internet, and telephones, videoconferencing does more than just bring scattered workers together. It also links remote schools in the Australian outback to teachers more than 930 mi. (1,500km) away.

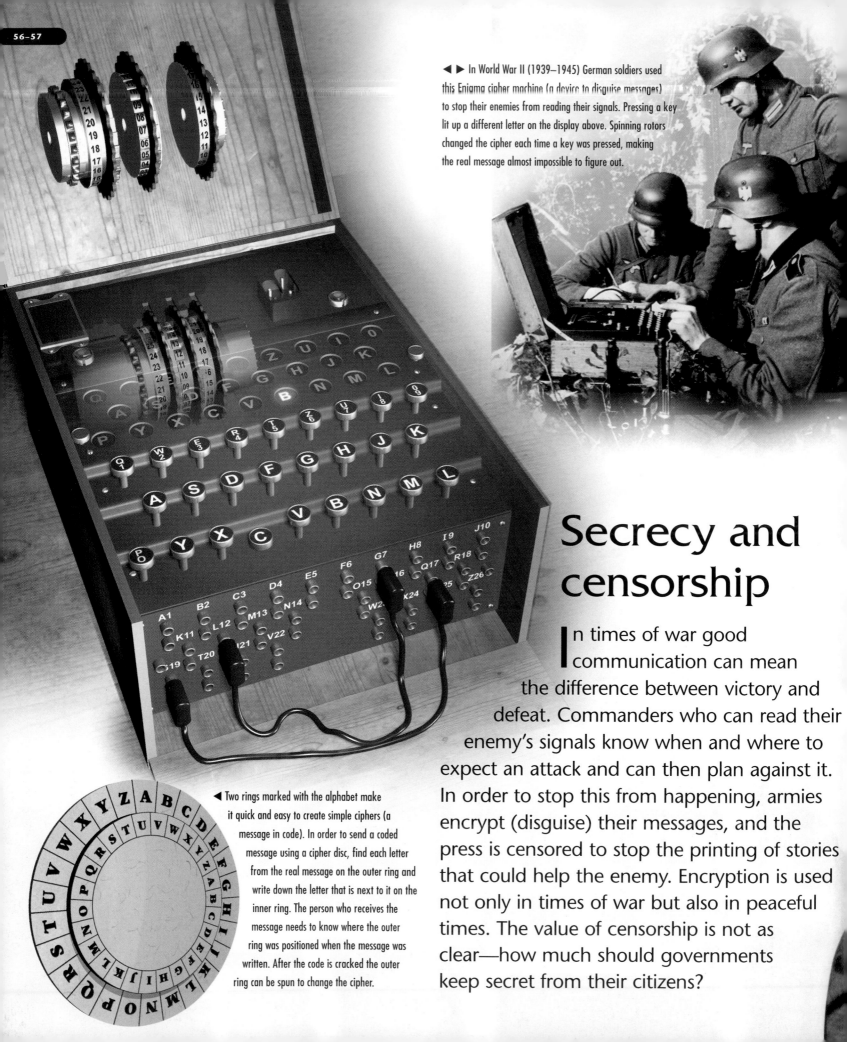

◄ ► In World War II (1939–1945) German soldiers used this Enigma cipher machine (a device to disguise messages) to stop their enemies from reading their signals. Pressing a key lit up a different letter on the display above. Spinning rotors changed the cipher each time a key was pressed, making the real message almost impossible to figure out.

Secrecy and censorship

In times of war good communication can mean the difference between victory and defeat. Commanders who can read their enemy's signals know when and where to expect an attack and can then plan against it. In order to stop this from happening, armies encrypt (disguise) their messages, and the press is censored to stop the printing of stories that could help the enemy. Encryption is used not only in times of war but also in peaceful times. The value of censorship is not as clear—how much should governments keep secret from their citizens?

◄ Two rings marked with the alphabet make it quick and easy to create simple ciphers (a message in code). In order to send a coded message using a cipher disc, find each letter from the real message on the outer ring and write down the letter that is next to it on the inner ring. The person who receives the message needs to know where the outer ring was positioned when the message was written. After the code is cracked the outer ring can be spun to change the cipher.

Invisible letters

Keeping communication secret is an ancient problem. One way to do it is to make the words invisible. Messages written with a pen dipped in lemon juice or urine disappear when the paper dries. Heating up the letter with an iron causes the words to appear.

Writing in cipher

Using a cipher to encrypt the message is a more reliable way to hide it from curious eyes. To use the simplest cipher, you swap each letter for the next one in the alphabet. For example "A" becomes "B," "L" turns into "M," and "I AM A SPY" would read "J BN B TQZ."

Cracking the code

Ciphers like this one are easy to unscramble if you know how they work. In English only the words "I" and "A" have just one letter. So in this message each of the two lone letters must be either an "I" or an "A." Two-letter words are also rare, so guessing "AM" would not be too difficult.

Simple codes are so easy to crack that they are no longer used to protect sensitive information. The ciphers that scramble credit card numbers for Internet shoppers are much more advanced, and deciphering them might take years, even with the fastest desktop computers.

The need for censorship

Everyone agrees that banking details, military information, and airline security methods have to be kept secret. This protects a country from enemies, so governments censor news reports that reveal these details. However, it is not easy to be sure about other types of information. Some governments try to stop newspapers from publishing stories that reveal government mistakes and corruption or that question leaders' decisions.

▲ A padlock symbol appears on secure web pages, showing that only trusted people can read what you have keyed in.

Freedom of speech

This type of censorship threatens the freedom of speech. Without freedom of speech, citizens cannot be sure that their politicians are honest and trustworthy. For example, in 1971 the U.S. government tried to censor the *Pentagon Papers*. These revealed facts about U.S. involvement in the Vietnam War. After a two-week court battle newspapers won the right to publish them.

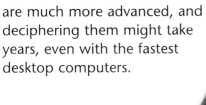

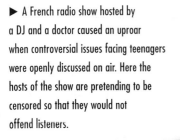

▶ A French radio show hosted by a DJ and a doctor caused an uproar when controversial issues facing teenagers were openly discussed on air. Here the hosts of the show are pretending to be censored so that they would not offend listeners.

Advertising

How many advertisements do you see and hear every day? You can try keeping track, but you will soon lose count. Most of us see up to 1,000 advertisements each day on television, in newspapers, and on the street. Even in movies, which seem to be free of commercials, advertisers pay to put famous brands in front of the camera. We cannot escape advertising—and maybe we should not try because it pays for the cost of much of our entertainment.

A word from our sponsor . . .

Advertising began hundreds of years ago when merchants painted signs to attract passersby to their stores. In the 1900s television and radio gave advertisers new ways to catch the attention of millions of people.

Today advertising plays a vital role in keeping communication flowing. Advertisers pay to promote their products, and thanks to this income, it costs us less to read publications and to receive television and radio shows. Some entertainment, such as commercial television, could not exist without advertisements. As more of us reach for the remote control during commercial breaks, advertisers have found ways to sneak their products into the plotlines of TV shows.

Cool or corrupting?

Although everyone likes getting something for nothing, advertising is not always a good thing. Commercials can persuade us to buy things we do not need. They also encourage us to start harmful habits such as smoking or overeating. So in most countries advertising is controlled by laws to ensure that the advertisements do not harm vulnerable people.

▲ Brands are special combinations of names, colors, and shapes that make products easy to spot on the shelf and easy to advertise. Brands stand out even when written in a different alphabet—can you identify this brand of soda?

▼ Advertising brightens up dull city views and has made places, such as New York City's Times Square, famous for their bright lights. But advertising laws control where these signs appear because nobody wants to see neon reflected in a beautiful lake.

SUMMARY OF CHAPTER 4: THE GLOBAL VILLAGE

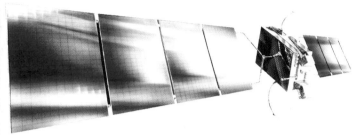

Inventing the future

Clever and imaginative science fiction writers, such as Arthur C. Clarke, predicted today's wired world long before the technology to make it possible even existed. Today we rely on satellites for countless communication tasks, including telephone calls, television broadcasts, and navigation signals.

Another communication technology—the Internet— began as a military command system. At one end there were radar dishes that warned of a nuclear attack, and at the other end were deadly missiles for counterattacks. Fortunately the missiles were never used, and the computer network that controlled them was turned to peaceful purposes. The network linked researchers and connected computers scattered around the globe.

The Web's friendly face

It took special software to make the Internet user-friendly. The "World Wide Web" was created in the 1990s when engineer Tim Berners-Lee became impatient with computers that could not "talk" to each other. He invented a point-and-click interface so that anyone could find anything anywhere on the growing network. Together Berners-Lee's Web browser and Ray Tomlinson's 1971 e-mail invention have made the Internet a popular success.

Controlling information and keeping data private on the Internet are problems. However, these are not new challenges. Censorship is as old as news itself. Ciphers, which are used to hide credit card details on the Web, began more than 2,000 years ago.

The services we use on the Internet seem free, but we still pay for them by viewing the advertisements that pop up on many Web pages. Not only does advertising pay for these Web pages, but it also cuts the cost of many other broadcast and printed media. Without advertisements, we would pay a lot more for our magazines, newspapers, movies, and television shows.

Go further . . .

Track communication satellites in orbit around Earth: www.science.nasa.gov/realtime/jtrack

Hear the inventor of the World Wide Web talking about his work: www.smithsonianassociates.org/programs/berners-lee/berners-lee.asp

View a time line of computer history: www.computerhistory.org

Behind the Media: Advertising by Catherine Chambers (Heinemann Library, 2002)

Secret Codes for Kids by Robert Allen (Scholastic, 2000)

Advanced ink scientist
Develops the inks that can be made to appear or change color under the control of a computer.

Mathematician
Employed by national security organizations to devise secure ciphers for protecting sensitive information and to decrypt enemy ciphers.

Satellite ground station technician
Helps operate and maintain the ground equipment that sends data to and from an orbiting satellite.

Web designer
Creates Web pages that aim to make online media as interesting and easy to use as their printed equivalent.

The National Cryptologic Museum gives a glimpse into the world of codes from the National Security Agency:
Baltimore-Washington Parkway
Baltimore, MD
Phone: (301) 688-5849
www.nsa.gov/museum

Find out how British cryptographers from World War II unraveled the "unbreakable" Enigma cipher:
Bletchley Park
Bletchly, England MK3 6EB
Phone: 44 1908 640404
www.bletchleypark.org.uk

Visit the American Advertising museum: www.admuseum.org

Glossary

abroad
In another country.

amplify
To make louder.

ARPANET
A computer network set up in the 1960s by the U.S. Department of Defense Advanced Research Projects Agency (ARPA) to allow universities to share information.

bass
The lower notes in music.

beacon
A raised structure that sends out messages such as radio signals.

broadcast
A radio or television signal that is transmitted over a wide area for many people to receive.

CAT scans
A way of building a detailed picture of what is inside the body by passing it through a narrow beam of X-rays.

censored
Prevented from broadcasting or printing facts because they may assist a country's enemy or embarrass leaders and powerful people.

ciphers
A method of changing messages so that only trusted people can understand them—to others the messages look like nonsense.

culture
The things that a group of people believe, do, and create that together make them different from other groups of people.

cuneiform
A form of writing made by pressing a wedge-shaped reed into wet clay.

cutting (film or video)
The removing and rearranging of shots to make a better show.

data
The information or facts stored on a computer.

develop (a photograph)
To make visible a picture recorded on film in a camera.

digital
Made up of a long series of on-off signals to be read by a computer.

dumb
Unable to speak.

emboss
To press a pattern into a surface.

encrypt
To encode a message using a cipher in order to make it unreadable to others.

etch
To burn or scratch a pattern into a surface.

exchange
A place where telephone calls are connected.

fossils
The impressions of long-dead plants or animals formed when stone has replaced their tissues.

freedom of speech
The right to say what you think, even if you disagree with your country's government.

infrared beams
The invisible rays that share some of the properties of both light and heat.

live performance
A performance for an audience broadcast or recorded from beginning to end without stopping.

magnetic field
The force that exists around a magnet and that attracts iron or steel objects.

magnetized
Made magnetic.

media
The many ways of communicating with large numbers of people, including television, radio, magazines, and newspapers.

missile
A flying weapon used to attack a distant enemy.

mixing (music)
Blending together the sound of two records so that their rhythms match.

modem
A device that converts signals into smooth waves that can travel down telephone lines.

motor neurone disease
An illness that kills the nerves that make the body's muscles move.

MP3
A way of compressing (squeezing) a digital sound recording so that it can be stored very efficiently— or a recording stored in this way.

network
A group of linked communication machines such as telephones or computers.

online
Connected to a computer network.

operator (telephone network)
A person who connects the caller to the person receiving the call.

orbiting
Circling in space.

pamphlets
Printed information that appears on a few loosely attached pages.

pitch
The scale of high to low sounds.

publisher
A person or company that organizes book, magazine, or newspaper production and distribution.

riff
A few notes that are played over and over to provide a rhythmical backing for music.

SAGE
Semiautomatic Ground Environment—the world's first computer network that controlled the U.S. missile defense system in the 1950s.

scratching (DJ)
Moving a record turntable by hand to play the same section of a track over and over again.

silicon chip
A miniaturized electronic circuit that replaces thousands or millions of individual parts.

speech synthesizer
An electronic device that imitates the sound of a human voice.

spools (film)
A pair of discs or frames held apart by a small tube and used for winding up film or videotape.

stammer
A speech impediment where sufferers repeat the beginning of a word.

Stone Age
A prehistoric period before people had learned how to make metal tools.

treaty
An agreement often between two or more countries.

universe
Everything in space, including the stars, the Sun, and Earth.

Web browsers
The computer software that displays pictures, text, and sound and organizes them into pages on-screen.

Index

Acknowledgments

The publisher would like to thank the following for permission to reproduce their material.
Every care has been taken to trace copyright holders. However, if there have been unintentional
omissions or failure to trace copyright holders, we apologize and will, if informed, endeavor
to make corrections in any future edition.

Key: *b* = bottom, *c* = center, *l* = left, *r* = right, *t* = top

Cover / Corbis; Cover *c* Getty; Cover *r* Getty; 1 SPL; 2 Corbis; 8*tl* Corbis; 8–9 Getty; 9*br* Corbis;
10 SPL; 11*t* SPL; 11*cr* SPL; 11*br* SPL; 12–13 Corbis; 12*tr* SPL;12*b* SPL; 13*b* Mary Evans Picture Library
(MEPL); 14*tl* Art Archive; 14*tr* Art Archive; 15*tl* Art Archive; 15*r* Art Archive; 16*tl* SPL; 17*b* Art Archive;
18*br* Corbis; 19*tr* Corbis; 19*b* British Museum; 20–21 Corbis; 20*tr* Corbis; 21*br* Corbis; 22–23 Art
Archive; 22*cr* Corbis; 23*br* Alamy; 24 MEPL; 24–25 U.S. Library of Congress; 25*bl* Corbis; 25*r* Corbis;
26–27 Corbis; 27*tl* U.S. Library of Congress; 28 Science and Society Picture Library; 29*t* MEPL;
29*tl* Corbis; 29*br* Corbis; 31 SPL; 32*tl* Corbis; 33*r* Corbis; 34 Corbis; 35 Corbis; 36*l* Getty;
36–37*t* Corbis; 37*tr* Getty; 38*tl* Corbis; 38*cl* Corbis; 38*bl* Getty; 38–39 Getty; 40*t* Rex Features;
41*b* Corbis; 42*tl* Getty; 42*bl* Kobal; 43*br* SPL; 44–45*b* Corbis; 45*tr* SPL; 46–47 Corbis; 49 SPL;
50*bl* SPL; 51*t* SPL; 51*cr* SPL; 51*br* SPL; 52l Alamy; 52–53 Alamy; 53*tl* Corbis; 54 Alamy;
55*tr* Alamy; 55*bl* Corbis; 55*br* Corbis; 56*tr* Corbis; 57*b* Corbis; 58*tl* Corbis;
58 Corbis; 59 SPL; 61 Art Archive; 62 Corbis; 64 MEPL

The publisher would like to thank the following illustrators:
Chris Molan 26*tl*; Jurgen Ziewe 4*bl*; 22*t*; 23*t*; 30*tl*; 33*b*; 40*bl*; 44*tl*; 52*tl*; 58*tl*;
Mike Davis 18*tl*; 29*bl*; 32*cr*; 47*br*; 58*bl*; 59*tr*

The author would like to dedicate this book to his sister, Julie.